SO YOU THINK YOU KNOW THE

Clive Gifford

a division of Hodder Headline Limited

© Hodder Children's Books 2004

Published in Great Britain in 2004
by Hodder Children's Books

Editor: Hayley Leach
Design by Fiona Webb
Cover design: Hodder Children's Books

10 9 8 7 6 5 4 3 2 1

ISBN: 0340881917

Printed by Bookmarque Ltd, Croydon, Surrey

The paper and board used in this paperback by
Hodder Children's Books are natural recyclable
products made from wood grown in sustainable forests.
The manufacturing processes conform to the
environmental regulations of the country of origin.

Hodder Children's Books
a division of Hodder Headline Limited
338 Euston Road
London NW1 3BH

Contents

Introduction

S o you think you know all there is to know
about the swinging sixties? Think you can
remember all the fads, fashions, fun, films, foods
and frolics? Contained in this book are over
1,000 questions covering many aspects of
sixties memories from the arrival of Action Man
to the tunes of the Zombies. Here's hoping
you manage to turn on and tune in to the
questions but don't drop out when it comes
to summoning up the answers.

Biography

Clive Gifford is an award-winning writer and
journalist with over 50 books in print including
The Living World, Eyewitness Guide: Media
and *The Water Puppets*, a children's novel set
during the Vietnam War.

Clive was captain of the Stanwell Secondary
School team who won their regional,
untelevised heat of *Top of the Form* but a
technicians strike prevented his side from
making their TV debut. Two years earlier, his
school had appeared on *Crackerjack* but
only girls were chosen to play for prizes. As
an adult, Clive has consoled himself by
compiling and writing several quiz books
including *So You Think You Know Harry Potter?*
and *The Family Flip Quiz*, and he has worked
as an editor on the *Who Wants to be a
Millionaire?* quiz books.

fun and Games

1. Which girls' doll featured extensive wardrobes, vehicles and a boyfriend called Ken?

2. If you accused Miss White in the Ballroom with the lead piping, what game were you playing?

3. Which game put people in contortions after they followed instructions from a spinning dial?

4. Which game saw a contestant win $700 for successfully removing a broken heart?

5. Which game featured a diver, a bathtub and a boot suspended from a lamppost?

6. The first World Championship for which racing toy took place in London in 1964?

7. Which game featured 30 sticks and 32 marbles?

8. What was the name of the flying disc that became a popular outdoor pastime in Britain during the sixties?

9. What make of toy truck was usually yellow and advertised by an elephant standing on it?

10. Which of the following two were not a spinning top found in the Battling Tops game: Whizzing Willy, Smarty Smitty, Twirling Tim, Hurricane Hank or Spinning Sammy?

11. Which artistic toy featured two knobs, one controlling vertical movement and the other horizontal?

12. What was the name of the Sindy doll's male friend?

13. The end of the sixties saw the introduction of the Space Hopper that was available in orange and which other colour?

14. Which girls' doll cried and wet herself after being fed by her small bottle?

15. What geometric drawing toy, complete with translucent plastic circles, became popular in the mid-1960s?

16. Which of the following items came with the original Action Man soldier figure: a training manual, identity tags, a bazooka, an equipment manual or a beret?

17. Who was the singing star on the cover of the 1963 *Boyfriend* annual: Cliff Richard, Dion or Tommy Steele?

18. Airfix Dogfight Doubles kits were made to what scale: 1/72, 1/120 or 1/32 scale?

19. If you collected a 'get out of jail free' card, what game would you have been playing?

20. What was the name of the American equivalent to the Action Man figure?

21. How many inches high were the official Beatles dolls sold in 1964: two inches, ten inches or five inches?

22. How much was the Corgi 007 Aston Martin DB5 when it was released in 1965: seven shillings, ten shillings, twelve shillings and sixpence or one guinea?

23. What item of Batman's clothing, which came complete with handcuffs, was first on many boys' Christmas lists in the 1960s?

24. Which doll was Britain's best-selling toy in 1961: Barbie, Pinocchio, Noddie or Sindy?

25. How many coloured quadrants were there on a Twister board?

26. What colour was the arena used in Battling Tops?

27. What plastic brick set introduced its first ever space-related toy in the 1960s?

28. What coloured modelling clay could be shaped with the additional Fun Factory?

29. Spirograph, Scalextric, Space Hopper or Battling Tops was voted Toy of the Year in 1967?

30. Which Grand Prix motor racing driver was used to promote Scalextric: Graham Hill, Emerson Fittipaldi, Jim Clark or Stirling Moss?

31. Which toy made its first appearance in 1964 complete with plastic moustache, hat and eyes, and has since appeared in the recent *Toy Story* movies?

32. By what other name were Instant Fish, often sold with a tiny aquarium, known?

33. Although some vehicles came and went, how many cars did the Matchbox line-up of vehicles always contain?

34. How many triple word score spaces were there on a standard Scrabble board?

35. And what colour were they?

36. What innovation occurred to Subbuteo footballers in the early sixties: players were made three-dimensional, were given fuzzy hair or had interchangeable shirts?

37. Can you name the three male Cluedo suspects?

38. In the Mouse Trap game, when the bucket was tipped, did the ball first travel down the wooden staircase, roll down the diving board or drop onto the see-saw?

39. Which of the following was not a weapon in Cluedo: dagger, candlestick, hammer, revolver or lead piping?

40. Which girls' doll came in a box which opened out to form a bath?

41. What colour was a one pound note in the 1960s version of Monopoly?

42. What was the warm name of the American toy car series which was a rival to Matchbox and Corgi in the late 1960s?

43. What colour was the body of an Etch-a-Sketch?

44. 1969 saw the introduction of movable eagle eyes on an Action Man: true or false?

45. Corgi's Thrush-Buster car, available in blue or white, was derived from which popular TV action show?

46. How many suspects were there in the standard Cluedo game?

47. Which one of the following was not a body part in the Operation game: Charlie Horse, Water on the Knee, Brain Ache or Butterflies in the Stomach?

48. Can you name the three female Cluedo suspects?

49. What craft was hidden inside the Thunderbird 2 model?

50. What colour was the zipped suit supplied with the first Action Man pilot figure?

Music

1. Which British female singer of the sixties was born Priscilla White and worked as a cloakroom attendant at the famous Cavern Club?

2. Jerry Garcia and Bob Weir were members of which late sixties band?

3. What was the name of the drummer Ringo Starr replaced in the Beatles?

4. Which of the following bands were not present at Woodstock: the Who, Genesis, Santana, Yes, or Sly and the Family Stone?

5. Which psychedelic group released a rare single, 'See Emily Play', in 1967?

6. Which DJ introduced the first ever edition of *Top of the Pops*: Simon Dee, Jimmy Saville or Tony Blackburn?

7. Who was the first solo British female singer to notch-up three number one hits in the 1960s: Cilla Black, Sandie Shaw, Lulu or Jackie Trent?

8. Steed and Gale, from the TV show *The Avengers*, released a 1964 single about what item of clothing?

9. Which innovative guitarist began his career working as a backing musician for singers including Little Richard?

10. Which pirate radio station was named after John F. Kennedy's daughter and broadcast from an old passenger ferry?

11. How many consecutive Beatles singles reached number one from 1962 onwards?

12. Which former guitarist from John Mayall's Bluesbreakers replaced Brian Jones in the Rolling Stones?

13. Which band had hits with 'Needles and Pins' and 'Don't Throw Your Love Away'?

14. 'If Paradise is Half as Nice' was a hit for the Honeycombs, Amen Corner, the Standells, or Terry Knight and the Pack?

15. Which of the following were not pirate radio stations in the mid-1960s: Radio Invicta, Radio England, Radio Emerald, Radio King or Radio Jackson?

16. Who was the innovative record producer sometimes known as the 'fifth Beatle'?

17. Which blues guitarist left John Mayall's Bluesbreakers to form Fleetwood Mac?

18. The Who never had a number one single in the 1960s: true or false?

19. Who sang 'Puppet on a String' to record the UK's first Eurovision Song Contest win in the sixties?

20. Tom Jones sang the title song to which Bond film?

21. Did Cliff Richard's 'Congratulations' ever win the Eurovision Song Contest?

22. 'My Old Man's a Dustman' was a number one hit in 1960 for which skiffle artist?

23. 'Walk Right Back' and 'Cathy's Clown' were number one hits for which pair of brothers?

24. Who out of the following was not a member of the Monkees: Mike Nesmith, Peter Tosh, Mickey Dolenz, Mike Berry or David Jones?

25. Which *Are You Being Served*? actress had a number one single with Mike Sarne in 1962, called 'Come Outside'?

26. B Bumble and the Stingers had a novelty number one single with which instrumental piece?

27. Which Beatles track gave the band their first Christmas number one single?

28. Which rock 'n' roll magazine appeared for the first time in 1967?

29. What was the name of the Herman's Hermits' lead singer?

30. Which band recorded *The Hangman's Beautiful Daughter* and *5000 Spirits or the Layers of the Onion* albums in the late 1960s?

31. Which member of the Rolling Stones died in 1969?

32. Which song, turned down by Sandie Shaw, gave Tom Jones his first hit record?

33. Who sang about two little boys called Joe and Jack and stayed at number one for six weeks as a result?

34. 'Crying in the Chapel' was a lesser-known number one hit for which male singer?

35. Which female singer sang with Big Brother and the Holding Company?

36. Which power trio featured the drumming of Ginger Baker and Jack Bruce on bass and vocals?

37. Which singing duo was first known as Tom and Jerry?

38. Berry Gordy, Joe Meek or Phil Spector founded the Tamla Motown record label?

39. Which famous US band were formerly known as Carl and the Passions?

40. Who sang the title song to the Bond film *From Russia With Love*?

41. Which Dylan song was filmed featuring him discarding a series of placards with lyric fragments and statements scrawled upon them?

42. What was the name of the 1968 film featuring the Monkees and co-written and co-produced by Jack Nicholson?

43. Which Beatles album, the band's seventh, featured: 'Eleanor Rigby', 'Tomorrow Never Knows' and 'Taxman'?

44. 'Those Were the Days My Friend' was a hit for Lulu, Mary Hopkin or Jackie Trent?

45. Which easy listening singer had hits with 'Distant Drums' and 'I Love You Because'?

46. Which Wall of Sound producer worked with artists including the Righteous Brothers, Ike and Tina Turner, the Ronettes and the Crystals?

47. Can you name either of the famous bands that US folk group the Mugwumps spawned when they split?

48. Which radio station started broadcasting off the Suffolk coast in March 1964?

49. Which member of the Beatles' entourage died in 1967?

50. Van Morrison fronted which late 1960s band from Belfast, who had a major hit with 'Here Comes the Night'?

Kids' Television

1. If it was Friday and five to five, what show was on the BBC?

2. Which popular TV puppet show finished being shown on the BBC in 1968 but was later broadcast on ITV?

3. What was the name of the *Wacky Races* car with the race number 2?

4. What colour was Lady Penelope's Rolls Royce in *Thunderbirds*?

5. Liberace played *Batman* villain, Fingers: true or false?

6. When the *Banana Splits* rocked, who played drums?

7. Which regular panel member of *Jukebox Jury* left in order to launch children's show *Magpie,* in 1968?

8. Who lived at Colley Mill just outside the village of Camberwick Green?

9. Pippin and Tog were characters in *Tales of the Riverbank*, *Pogle's Wood* or *Trumpton*?

10. What was the name of Sandy Ricks' dolphin friend?

11. Which of the following was not a character in *The Herbs*: Sage the Owl, Constable Knapweed, Aunt Mint, Uncle Oregano or Lady Rosemary?

12. Who was the father of the sons who piloted the Thunderbirds' craft?

13. Who was the long-running presenter of *Animal Magic*?

14. *Tales of the Riverbank*, *Ivor the Engine* and *The Sagas of Noggin the Nog* all made their debut in which year of the sixties?

15. Lord Belborough's butler in Chigley was called Mr Fetch, Mr Brackett, Mr Clamp or Thomas Tripp?

16. Which *Stingray* character couldn't speak?

17. Which show featured tales starring Hammy the Hamster and Roderick the Rat?

18. Who ran Pippin Fort in *Camberwick Green*?

19. What was the name of the rag doll in *Play School*?

20. Did Captain Scarlet, Troy Tempest or Mike Mercury work for the World Aquanaut Security Patrol (WASP)?

21. Which cowardly sea captain sailed in the Black Pig?

22. Leslie Crowther and Peter Glaze were mainstays of which popular sixties children's show?

23. Prince Turhan and the magician, Farik, starred in which cartoon show?

24. Who was Lady Penelope's chauffeur?

25. What was the name of the first ever *Blue Peter* dog?

26. Jimmy Gibson and Professor Popkiss were goodies in which Gerry Anderson show?

27. The BBC banned *Pinky and Perky* in 1966 for being too political: true or false?

28. Which *Batman* villain did Zsa Zsa Gabor play?

29. What number was the Thunderbird craft orbiting in space and piloted by John Tracy?

30. Who was Andy Pandy's female companion?

31. Spotty Dog, Buttercup the Cow and Jenny were all characters in which puppet show?

32. Name either the clueless Police Commissioner or the Police Chief in the action show, *Batman*.

33. John Wayne played *Batman* villain, Mr Freeze: true or false?

34. What show, from the BBC's *Tales from Europe*, featured Princess Thousandbeauty: *The Singing Ringing Tree*, *The Pied Piper* or *Rapunzel*?

35. What old song did Huckleberry Hound frequently sing?

36. What was the name of the cat found in the same show as Pixie and Dixie?

37. Mike Mercury and his monkey, Mitch, fought Masterspy and Zarin in which animated show?

38. Which cartoon family lived at 342 Greasepit Terrace?

39. Which surreal animated show made its debut in 1965 in Britain and featured a hairy dog, a snail, a cow and a strange creature on a spring?

40. 'Like a streak of lightening flashing from the sky' were the opening words of which show's theme tune?

41. Who was the first male presenter of *Blue Peter* from 1958 to 1967?

42. What was the name of the gang which terrorised the *Banana Splits*?

43. What was the first name of the youngest of Jeff Tracy's sons who piloted Thunderbird 4?

44. What sort of creature was *The Herbs* character, Parsley?

45. Did Mrs Scrubit help Jenny Woodentop, Mummy Woodentop or Daddy Woodentop?

46. Lieutenant George 'Phones' Sheridan and Sub-Lieutenant Fisher starred in *Stingray*, *Fireball XL5* or *Supercar*?

47. What sort of creature was Idris in the *Ivor the Engine* children's TV show?

48. How many cats apart from Top Cat formed his gang?

49. Sarge and Meekley, Luke and Blubber and Peter Perfect were all members of which American cartoon show?

50. What was the name of the four-eyed boffin who assisted the Tracy brothers and International Rescue?

Fashion

1. Did mods, rockers or beatniks tend to own motor scooters in the mid-1960s?

2. Which female model was nicknamed the Shrimp?

3. Which street, which runs parallel to Regent's Street, became home of the Mod fashion movement in London during the 1960s?

4. Which young hairstylist became famous overnight for his geometrical bob haircuts?

5. Which influential French designer opened his Rive Gauche chain in 1966?

6. Who wore white go-go boots while singing 'These Boots Are Made for Walking' in 1966?

7. Which singer and actress. who starred in films such as *Move Over Darling* and *The Thrill of it All*, inspired the girl-next-door look?

8. Which fashion designer ran a chain of boutiques called Bazaar?

9. What shortened, wide-legged trouser became popular in the mid-1960s?

10. Which wife of an American President became a fashion trendsetter in the early 1960s?

11. What was the nickname of men's shoes which featured a long and pointed toe?

12. What male ankle-high footwear, with an elastic panel on the side, were named after a fashionable part of London?

13. Who started the Ginger Group fashion label in 1963?

14. Paco Rabanne caused a stir with a dress made of what material, in 1965?

15. What was the name of the straight, slim, hip-length jacket named after a former Indian Prime Minister?

16. What art movement influenced fashion with its use of trick optical effects of contrasting areas of black, white and colour?

17. What was the nickname of the necklace no hippie was without in the late 1960s?

18. Which chain of stores specialised in producing adult versions of young girls' clothes with knee-high socks, knitwear and peaked caps?

19. The Quorum boutique became famous for the designs of Betsey Johnson, Anne Fogarty or Ossie Clark?

20. Which road in Chelsea was a haven for fashion trendsetters in the 1960s?

21. British designer John Bates designed the costumes for the character of Emma Peel in which TV action show?

22. Which fashion designer opened his first of 160 stores in 1967?

23. Which futuristic film featured clothing designs by Jaques Fonteray and helped popularise the 'space age' look?

24. In what city did Barbara Hulaniki open her Biba boutique?

25. Model Jean Shrimpton had a relationship with which famous fashion photographer?

21

26. Which fashion designer accepted an OBE from the Queen in 1966, whilst wearing a miniskirt?

27. Teds of the sixties frequently wore a D.A. hairstyle, but what was D.A. short for?

28. What flower was used as a logo by Mary Quant?

29. Sandy Shaw inspired thousands of hippies not to wear what particular item of clothing?

30. Psychedellions were plastic flowers you clipped on to your handbag, sandals or hats?

31. The pill-box hat became popular in the early 1960s after which wife of a politician was seen wearing one on television?

32. Paisley print clothing was a popular choice of people who followed Merseybeat, Mod, Psychedelic or Soul music?

33. In 1968, dry cleaners started to charge by the inch for cleaning miniskirts: true or false?

34. I Was Lord Kitchener's Valet, was a store selling: fashionable underwear, vintage clothing, outrageous hats or beachwear?

35. Were stockings, bikinis or tights invented in the 1960s?

36. Which model was born in Neasden as Lesley Hornby?

37. What was the name of the long-haired coat which usually became foul smelling after a few festival outings?

38. Which skirt was the longest: the maxi, the mini or the midi?

39. What brand of medical sandal became fashionable for a period in the mid-1960s?

40. Who was known as Queen of the Mods, was a fashion icon for teenage girls and endorsed Cathy's Survival Kit, a portable make-up kit for girls?

41. London designer Mr Fish inspired the nickname of what clothing item which widened throughout the decade?

42. Which rock guitarist's Union Jack jacket inspired thousands of copies?

43. Which footballer opened his own clothing boutique called Edwardia, in Manchester?

44. The first fashion boutique in Carnaby Street offered fashions for children, men or women?

45. Lord John was the first boutique in Carnaby Street, Oxford Street, Soho or Kings Road?

46. Terence Conran opened his Habitat store in Holborn, Fulham, Whitechapel or Islington?

47. The Scott Paper Company introduced a paper piece of clothing which sold over half a million copies in 1966. What clothing item was it?

48. Were Emanuelle Khanh's frilly miniskirts part of the Op Art fashion movement, a French Ye Ye fashion?

49. 1967 was the year of the turtleneck sweater, tie-dye t-shirts or go-go boots according to the *Daily News Record* fashion magazine?

50. The lipstick radio was an invention of Mary Quant, Paco Rabanne or Biba?

TeLevision

1. Pike, Godfrey and Frazer were all soldiers in which BBC comedy show?

2. Who was the original host of *University Challenge*?

3. Britain's longest-running TV soap started in 1960. What was it?

4. PC Bert Lynch and PC 'Fancy' Smith were characters in which popular police drama?

5. In the late 1960s, the BBC testcard featured a girl and a doll playing what game?

6. ATV introduced which soap based on a motel in the Midlands in 1964?

7. Which 1960s BBC film about nuclear war was banned?

8. Who hosted both *Candid Camera* and the *Golden Shot* during the 1960s?

9. What was the name of the *Golden Shot's* crossbow controller?

10. Samantha Stevens and her daughter, Tabitha, were leading characters in which show first seen on BBC1 in 1967?

11. Who was the subject of the first TV interview with a member of the royal family in May 1961?

12. Which five minute long police and crime show was introduced by TV station ATV in 1961?

13. Barbara Perkins was the female lead in which spy action TV series?

14. Who portrayed a one legged actor applying for the role of Tarzan in a sixties comedy sketch?

15. What was the full title of the satire show frequently referred to as TW3?

16. Which of the following acts were on the first edition of *Top of the Pops*: the Hollies, the Shirelles, the Swinging Blue Jeans or Cliff Richard?

17. Which two of the following starred at the 1963 *Royal Variety Performance*: Cliff Richard, Pinky and Perky, the Beatles or the Bachelors?

18. The first televised *Royal Variety Performance* occurred in which year?

19. Which show made its debut in the early 1960s with teams from Reading to Leeds trying to answer 'answers for ten'?

20. Rag-and-bone man Harold and his Dad, Albert, starred in which classic sitcom?

21. Andrew Gardiner and Alastair Burnet were the hosts of which show which was first broadcast in July 1967?

22. Which spacecraft, with a registration of NCC-1701, was on a five-year mission?

23. What sci-fi show, co-written by astronomer Fred Hoyle, featured an android girl played by Julie Christie?

24. Which comedy, which made its debut in 1961, featured the trials and tribulations of Fenner Fashions?

25. Which British sitcom was based on the inhabitants of 24 Sebastopol Terrace?

26. Which Dr Who was the first to battle the Yeti and the Ice Warriors: the first, the second or the third?

27. Which medical drama, based in 1920s Scotland, featured Dr Cameron and Janet the housekeeper?

28. Which sci-fi puppet show featured Matt Matic and Zoonie the Lazoon?

29. *On the Braden Beat* was a sitcom, a consumer affairs programme, a police drama or a variety show?

30. In which year of the sixties did *Steptoe and Son* stop being produced, only to reappear in the 1970s?

31. In which show did three teams from different parts of Britain compete, play their joker, and try to win a place in a similar European competition?

32. The Beatle's first TV appearance was on *People and Places*; *Ready, Steady, Go*; the *Ed Sullivan Show* or *Top of the Pops*?

33. What night was *That Was the Week that Was* usually broadcast?

34. Which actor played the second Dr Who?

35. Which crossword-based quiz show was hosted by Bob Holness for 130 episodes from 1962 to 1964?

36. Who was the long-serving host of *Police 5*, which began in 1962?

37. Which American soap opera featured actors such as Mia Farrow and Ryan O'Neil and ran for over 500 episodes?

38. What *Star Trek* character did DeForrest Kelly play?

39. *Not So Much a Programme, More a Way of Life*, was the successor to which popular satire show?

40. Which character in *Dad's Army* was a butcher?

41. Which *Dad's Army* character was a spiv?

42. Who was the tallest member of the Monty Python team?

43. In which show in 1963 did Albert Tatlock and Alf Roberts end up in the cells after assaulting a policeman?

44. Which dance outfit did Pan's People replace on *Top of the Pops* in 1967?

45. Dusty Springfield was one of the acts on the very first *Top of the Pops* show: true or false?

46. Jimmy, Jimmy's flute called Freddie and the evil Witchiepoo starred in which surreal children's show?

47. Whose *Coronation Street* marriage to Steve Tanner in 1967 was watched by over 20 million people?

48. Which controversial 1969 sitcom saw Eric Sykes having to deal with Kevin O'Grady, a Pakistani worker played by Spike Milligan?

49. Meg Richardson had a son and a daughter in *Crossroads*. Can you name either of them?

50. Who played the female lead in the show *Sykes*?

Celebrities

1. Which twin brothers ran an East End crime ring and were convicted of the murder of Jack 'The Hat' McVitie?

2. Which high-ranking government official was at the centre of a sex scandal in 1963?

3. Which famous actress was found dead in her apartment in 1962?

4. Which musician produced a book called *In His Own Write*?

5. Which civil rights leader was awarded the Nobel Peace Prize in 1964?

6. Which revolutionary leader was killed in 1967?

7. Which East End photographer married actress Catherine Deneuve in 1965?

8. Which leader of the Conservative Party was well-known as a keen yachtsman and musician?

9. Which popstar married hairdresser Maureen Cox in 1965?

10. Albert De Salvo was the Boston Strangler, the Third Man or Malcolm X's assassin?

11. Which *Peyton Place* actress married Frank Sinatra?

12. Which former British Prime Minister died in 1965 and was buried amid much ceremony?

13. Which Italian model was the girlfriend of Rolling Stone Brian Jones and Keith Richards?

14. Which member of the Kennedy clan had a car accident on Chapaquiddick Island in which his passenger was killed?

15. Sirhan Sirhan was found guilty of shooting which US politician?

16. Who was killed on Coniston Water in the Lake District trying to break the world water speed record in 1967?

17. Which American comedian died of a morphine overdose in August 1966?

18. Which high-profile acting couple married, helped fund the HTV television station and starred together in the films, *The V.I.Ps*, *The Sandpiper* and *Boom!*, during the sixties?

19. Which popular and gifted footballer first played for Manchester United in 1963?

20. What was the name of Roman Polanski's wife killed by the Manson family?

21. In what year did Bob Dylan 'go electric', upsetting many of his fans?

22. Which artist married a model 45 years younger than himself in 1961?

23. In what year were the Kray twins jailed for murder?

24. Which right wing British politician made the 'rivers of blood' speech in 1968?

25. Which pirate radio star had a Saturday evening chat show on the BBC called *Dee Time*?

26. Peter Sellers married which Swedish actress in 1964?

27. In which year did John Lennon marry Cynthia Powell?

28. Which proponent of LSD use uttered the famous quote, 'Turn on, Tune in and Drop out'?

29. Who became the youngest MP in 1965 and later went on to lead the Liberal Party?

30. Which American actress starred in *Cat Ballou*, *They Shoot Horses Don't They* and *A Walk On the Wild Side*?

31. Who was the manager of the Rolling Stones?

32. Which wife of an ex-President married shipping magnate Aristotle Onassis in 1968?

33. Chas Chandler was Jimi Hendrix's manager, but which band had he played bass for?

34. Which female politician became Britain's Minister for Transport in the 1965 cabinet reshuffle?

35. Who was executed for the A6 murder in 1962?

36. Who was Fidel Castro's right-hand man during the Cuban revolution?

37. The singer of 'To Sir, with Love' married Bee Gee, Maurice Gibb, in 1969. Who was the singer?

38. Which radical black leader was assassinated in 1965?

39. Which Beatle had his tonsils removed in February 1969?

40. How many times had Elizabeth Taylor been married before she married Richard Burton?

41. In which city, on the tip of Southern Spain, did John Lennon and Yoko Ono marry in 1969?

42. Name two of the four stars of the satirical revue, *Beyond the Fringe*.

43. What was the name of the Eastern mystic who the Beatles studied under in India?

44. Which TV and radio comic actor committed suicide in Sydney, Australia, in 1968?

45. Which actress starred in *Bullit and the Deep*?

46. Who married George Harrison in 1966?

47. Patricia Krenwinkel, Leslie Van Houten and Susan Atkins were members of which cult group?

48. James Earl Ray was charged with the killing of Lee Harvey Oswald, Martin Luther King or Robert Kennedy?

49. Who captured world-land and world-water speed records in 1964?

50. Which folk singer, who recorded 'Farewell for Angelina' in 1965, was jailed twice for anti-war protests?

Events

1. In which French city were there mass student riots in 1968?

2. What was the name of the spy plane pilot shot down over the USSR in 1960?

3. A revolving restaurant was opened in London in 1966 on top of which building?

4. In which year did the Beatles make their first visit to the United States?

5. From which Asian nation did an epidemic of influenza come in 1968?

6. Which River Thames crossing opened in 1967?

7. Which country did a number of Arab nations fight in the Six Day War in 1967?

8. Brook Advisory Clinics were established in the 1960s for what purpose?

9. Who, in 1963, led a civil rights march of over 200,000 people?

10. Which American city was the destination of the civil rights march of 1963?

11. Which African nation was granted its independence from Britain in October 1960?

12. Which European country left NATO in 1966?

13. In which year did Britain suffer the 'Great Freeze'?

14. Which mountainous European country did not let women vote in elections until 1971?

15. Who shot and killed Lee Harvey Oswald?

16. In 1966, which spy escaped from his London prison?

17. Which American President announced he wouldn't seek re-election during the sixties?

18. Which seaside town saw the worst of the violence between mods and rockers during the 1964 May Bank holiday weekend?

19. Which famous boxer joined the Nation of Islam movement in 1964?

20. In 1967 a large outbreak of what disease eventually saw more than 400,000 farm animals killed?

21. Which European country switched to driving on the right in 1967?

22. What crime occurred on the 8th August 1963?

23. The Sharpeville Massacre occurred in which country?

24. In May 1968, ten million workers came out on strike in which European country?

25. In what year was the Palestine Liberation Organisation founded?

26. What sort of creatures were Chi-Chi and An-An?

27. To what part of Britain did the government send troops in 1969?

28. Which band was arrested for drugs, inspiring *The Times* to write a newspaper column condemning their treatment?

29. In what year did the International Lawn Tennis Association abolish the distinction between amateurs and professionals?

30. Which racehorse won the Cheltenham Gold Cup for three years in a row?

31. Which Italian city lost many of its art treasures due to flooding in 1966?

32. Which country tested its first atomic bomb in 1960 in the Sahara Desert?

33. Who became US President after John F. Kennedy was assassinated?

34. Robert Kennedy was assassinated in the same year as Martin Luther King: true or false?

35. Which soul singer was shot dead in 1964 by motel manageress Bertha Lee Franklin?

36. Who began a 44 day strike, starting in May 1966, which forced the UK government to declare a state of emergency?

37. What was the name of the tower block whose corner flats collapsed in 1968?

38. Which Apollo mission landed the first men on the moon?

39. In what year was abortion made legal in Britain?

40. Who was president of the USSR during the 1962 Cuban Missile Crisis?

41. Who was leader of the Vietminh in North Vietnam?

42. Who was elected US President in 1968?

43. Who was the third man in the Burgess and Maclean spy scandal?

44. At which Olympic Games were the black power salutes first seen?

45. In 1966, Britain banned all trade with which African nation?

46. Which band were onstage at Altamont when a man was killed by a band of Hell's Angels?

47. Which country detonated its first H-bomb in June 1967?

48. Which European city did President Kennedy make a historic visit to in 1963?

49. How much did the Great Train Robbers steal: 1.2, 1.8, 2.6 or 4.2 million pounds?

50. Which one of the following was not one of the Great Train Robbers: Ronnie Biggs, Charlie Wilson, Jack Fenshaw or Thomas Wisbey?

Music

1. Who was the youngest member of the Fab Four?

2. Bob Dylan had a number one single in the UK during the 1960s: true or false?

3. Who had a hit with the song, 'She's Not There'?

4. Which one of the following was not a regular panel member of *Juke Box Jury*: Pete Murray, Alma Cogan, Susan Stranks or Tony Blackburn?

5. Which British Rhythm and Blues band at different times featured Eric Clapton, Jimmy Page and Peter Green as guitarists?

6. Which female Motown artist covered Otis Redding's 'Respect' to gain her first major hit?

7. Tom and John Fogerty were members of which southern US band who had a 1969 hit with 'Proud Mary'?

8. The 1967 Marine Offences Act outlawed what sort of entertainment?

9. Jet Harris left which band in 1962 to be replaced by Brian 'Liquorice' Locking?

10. What late Beatles period song is the only one crediting a fifth member?

11. Which musician was the fifth member credited: Eric Clapton, Billy Ocean, Duane Allman or Ian Stewart?

12. Which UK band started out as the Drifters and became best known for their instrumental hits?

13. Who had an instrumental hit with 'Wipeout': Jan and Dean, the Surfaris or the Hondells?

14. Who released two albums in 1967, one of which was 'Are You Experienced'?

15. Which Beatles song was banned in 1967 by the BBC for its alleged drug references?

16. 'They're Coming To Take Me Away Ha-Haaa!' was a novelty hit for the Mad Hatters, Mad Montgomery, Napoleon XIV or the Nutters and Bolts?

17. Who released 'Strange Brew' and 'I Feel Free' as singles in 1967?

18. 'Telstar', 'Jack the Ripper' and 'Swinging Low' were all hit records produced by who?

19. 'River Deep, Mountain High' was a major hit for which husband and wife duo?

20. 'You've Lost That Lovin' Feeling' was a 1963 hit for which singing duet?

21. The Bee Gees were the second ever band to be played on Radio One: true or false?

22. 'Please, Please Me', 'I Saw Her Standing There' or 'Twist and Shout' was the first track on the Beatles' first ever album?

23. Which singer released 'The Last Waltz' and 'Release Me' in 1967?

24. Which support act was dropped from the 1967 Monkees tour for being too erotic?

25. Which one of the following was not a member of the Velvet Underground: Maureen Tucker, Lou Reed, John Prine or Sterling Morrison?

26. Which folk-rock band released 'Unhalfbricking' and 'Liege and Lief' in 1969?

27. What was the first year in the sixties that the UK won the Eurovision Song Contest?

28. Who fronted the Tijuana Brass?

29. The Rolling Stones, performing 'I Wanna Be Your Man', were the first band on *Juke Box Jury*, *Ready, Steady, Go* or *Top of the Pops*?

30. Which husband and wife team sang 'I Got You Babe' in 1965?

31. 'Young Girl' was a huge hit for: the 1910 Fruitgum Company, Gary Puckett and the Union Gap or the Scaffold?

32. Which former singer in the American group, the Drifters, had a major sixties hit with 'Stand By Me'?

33. Whose *Blue Hawaii* album spent 17 weeks at number one in the UK charts in 1960?

34. Which UK pop music show ran from 1963 to 1966 and featured Cathy McGowan as its best known presenter?

35. Where did the Rolling Stones play a large free festival just two days after Brian Jones' death?

36. Motown's first number one single was 'Please, Mr Postman'. Can you name the female vocal group who sang it?

37. Which song by the Byrds, was banned from BBC airplay for its references to drugs?

38. Which group were formerly a backing band for Ronnie Hawkins and later, Bob Dylan?

39. Which instrument did Stu Sutcliffe play with the Beatles, albeit not very well?

40. Which fashion designer did singer Sandie Shaw marry in March 1968?

41. Which sixties band had hits with 'Shapes of Things', 'For Your Love' and 'Heart Full of Soul'?

42. Whose 1966 double album was called *Freak Out*?

43. On which Beatles album were found the tracks, 'Eight Days a Week', 'No Reply' and 'I'm a Loser'?

44. What small rock and pop venue moved in 1964 from Oxford Street onto Wardour Street in London?

45. What was the name of Frank Zappa's band on his early albums?

46. Which early 1960s dance move was popularised by a Chubby Checker single?

47. Whose album, *Ogden Nuts Gone Flake*, was sold in a pretend tobacco tin?

48. Can you complete the name of the following Merseybeat band, Billy J. Kramer...?

49. Muff and Steve Winwood were brothers who had a huge hit with 'Keep on Running', with which group?

50. Which singer was known as 'Soul Brother Number One' and released albums, *Live at the Apollo* and *Pure Dynamite! Live at the Royal* during the sixties?

Life

1. What station would you find by tuning in your radio to 208 metres?

2. How many old pennies were there to a shilling?

3. Which London Underground line opened in 1969?

4. What was no longer free in secondary schools from 1968 onwards?

5. Which fast-moving *Beano* character made his first appearance in 1964: Sammy the Speed, Billy Whizz or Roger the Dodger?

6. What sort of shops became legal in Britain in 1961?

7. Button-controlled pedestrian crossings appeared in 1962. Were they nicknamed Panda, Pelican or Parrot crossings?

8. What unusually-shaped coin made its first appearance in 1969?

9. Which of the following girls' comics was not published in the 1960s: *Bunty, The Girlfriend, Misty* or *Judy*?

10. What were Corby, Telford and Bracknell examples of in the 1960s?

11. What was the name of the trading stamps given out by supermarkets such as Tesco, throughout the 1960s?

12. What became the new maximum road speed limit in 1965?

13. Which TV-based comic included a comic strip of Daktari and Magnus Robot Fighter?

14. Rona Munro was the original author of which set of reading scheme books featuring two children whose names began with the same letter?

15. Purchase Tax was replaced by what new tax during the sixties?

16. What food item came with a lion stamped on it until 1968?

17. Which female character, similar to Dennis the Menace, entertained readers of *The Beano* throughout the sixties?

18. How many shillings were there to a pound?

19. What new town of the sixties became the home of the Open University?

20. What choice was offered for the first time to people who posted letters in 1968?

21. In 1968, the London County Council was replaced by which body?

22. Which boys' comic featured Dan Dare and his battles against the Mekons?

23. How many shillings were there to a guinea?

24. In what year were the last National Servicemen called up?

25. In the late sixties, what radio station would you find on the dial at 247 metres?

26. What was first issued in London in 1960: parking tickets, premium bonds or 50 pound banknotes?

27. What was the name of the comic which featured all the Gerry Anderson TV shows including *Thunderbirds*?

28. In what town did Britain's first legal casino open in 1962?

29. What change occurred to your postal address from 1966 onwards?

30. Were pyramid-shaped blocks of flavoured ice in a paper pack called: Jubblies, Polar Pyramids or Ice Triangles?

31. If your parents drove a Velox or Victor, what make of car did they own?

32. Which coin was no longer legal tender after 1961?

33. Which comic character, who appeared in both *Boys' World* and *The Eagle*, was bullied and weedy until he wore new spectacles which gave him super powers?

34. What did motorists have to put their cars through for the first time from 1960 onwards?

35. In 1964, which tube station became the first with an automatic ticket barrier: Stamford Brook, Hatton Cross, Pimlico or Leicester Square?

36. Which black and white banknote ceased to be legal tender in 1969?

37. Which British broadsheet-format comic included the Numbskulls, and Pop, Dick and Harry among its comic strips?

38. What Lyons Maid product, linked to *Thunderbirds*, featured vanilla ice cream, strawberry ice and had its top dipped in chocolate and hundreds and thousands?

39. What sort of thing was Anglo Beat Mint: food flavouring, chewing gum, toothpaste or lavatory cleaner?

40. What was the most popular burger bar chain in the UK in the 1960s?

41. What was the minimum school-leaving age in the sixties?

42. What test for motorists was introduced by law in 1967?

43. What symbols were first seen at petrol stations from 1967 onwards?

44. Which *Beano* character was first joined by a rare Abyssinian Wire-haired Tripe Hound in 1963?

45. Which company introduced a range of small-wheeled bicycles, handy for commuting adults, in the early 1960s?

46. Peter and Jane were the characters in one set of learn-to-read books but what was the name of their dog?

47. Which children's TV hero got his own comic at the start of 1969 costing 8d: the Lone Ranger, Zorro, Joe-90 or Sherlock Holmes?

48. Which boys' comic featured the Steel Commando, Sylvester and the Touchstone, and Robot Archie?

49. David 'Kid' Jensen joined which independent radio station, popular with teenagers, in 1968?

50. Which ice lolly was introduced by Lyons Maid in 1963 for 6d and featured a multi-flavoured rocket shape?

TeLeVision

1. Which popular panel game featured Robert Morley and Frank Muir as the original team captains?

2. Charlie Barlow, Inspector Bamber and John Watt were characters later introduced into which popular TV police series?

3. *The Fugitive* portrayed a man on the run after being wrongly convicted of a murder. What was the character's name?

4. What American comedy series featured a journalist character called Tim O'Hara, who passes-off an alien from Mars as his Uncle Martin?

5. Which legendary comic duo often appeared in flat caps and macs talking over pints of beer in their 1965-66 show?

6. What satire, sketch and song show was presented by John Bird, Robert Robinson and Lynda Baron: *BBC 3*, *That Was the Week that Was*, *Not Only – But Also* or *The Walrus and the Carpenter*?

7. Bob Ferris and Terry Collier were the stars of which comedy show, which began airing in 1964?

8. Who did *Coronation Street's* Ken Barlow marry in 1962?

9. Who was the original presenter of *World of Sport*?

10. Against which adversary was the original Dr Who fighting before he regenerated into the second Dr Who?

11. *Steptoe and Son* lived in Rags Row, Oildrum Lane, Cardboard Crescent or Boxcart Avenue?

12. Diana Ross and the Supremes were the stars of which year's *Royal Variety Performance*?

13. Which show featured crime fighter Simon Templar?

14. Which western was set around Shiloh Ranch and featured Trampas and Judge Henry Garth?

15. What was the name of the *That Was the Week that Was* singer, who sang the amusing closing song of the show?

16. Which show featured honest copper George, his son-in-law, Andy Crawford, and Desk Sergeant Finch?

17. Charlie Drake starred as an unemployable character at a labour exchange in which programme?

18. Which adversary of Dr Who created the Daleks?

19. Which infamous arrivals to *Coronation Street* moved into number 13 in 1964?

20. Which American TV show featured Clint Eastwood playing Rowdy Yates?

21. Which actor played the first Dr Who making his debut in 1963?

22. Name two of the three Avenger actresses who played alongside John Steed.

23. Which show closed with Peter Cook and Dudley Moore singing, 'Goodbye'?

24. What was Captain James T. Kirk's middle name?

25. Which show featured a dead man in a white suit called Marty?

26. Who was the first presenter of *Tomorrow's World*?

27. What was the profession of the original Dr Who's first two assistants?

28. Which contact sport occupied almost an hour of *World of Sport* on a Saturday afternoon?

29. Arthur Negas introduced which panel game show about antiques?

30. Which American sitcom featured a millionaire and his wife, a professor, an actress, a skipper and a farm girl?

31. Which part of *Bewitched's* Samantha Steven's body did she move to cast a spell?

32. What was the occupation of Samantha's husband, Darrin, in *Bewitched*?

33. In *Adam Adamant Lives!* who was the hero's arch-enemy: the Face, the Hooded Claw or the Eve Machine?

34. Which sitcom featured comic actors: John Le Mesurier, Peggy Mount and Sid James?

35. Which spin-off series from *Z Cars* starred Stratford Johns as Barlow, and Frank Windsor as Inspector Watt?

36. Who controlled the USS Enterprise's engine room?

37. Which one of the following shows did not feature Spike Milligan: *Curry and Chips*, *The World of Beachcomber*, *Do Not Adjust Your Set* or *Q5*?

38. Which sporting event was broadcast on both ATV and BBC, and was watched by approximately 33 million people?

39. What soap opera motel was blown up by a World War II bomb in 1967?

40. Which popular TV singer and comedian used to shake his hands and say, 'I wanna tell you a story'?

41. Fenn Street Secondary Modern was the setting for which 1968 show brought to the screens by London Weekend Television?

42. Sketches featuring John Cleese, Tim Brooke-Taylor, Marty Feldman and Graham Chapman appeared in which comedy programme?

43. Which make of car did *The Saint* always drive?

44. Edward Woodward played a reluctant secret service agent and hitman in which show?

45. What was the name of the TV show featuring *Goon Show* radio scripts performed by puppets?

46. What was the name of the hand-held weapon deployed by the *Star Trek* crew?

47. Name either of the top agents of the United Network Command for Law Enforcement whose adventures thrilled viewers from the mid-sixties onwards.

48. What football team did *'Til Death Do Us Part's* Alf Garnett support?

49. Which of the following were part of the team of the original *World of Sport* commentators and presenters: Jimmy Hill, Kenneth Wolstenholme, Freddie Truman or Henry Cooper?

50. What was the biggest ratings puller of 1966: *The London Palladium Show, Miss World, Secombe and Friends* or *The Avengers*?

Arts and Entertainment

1. Which satirical magazine first appeared in 1962?

2. Which poet and leading light in the Beat Movement wrote *Howl*?

3. Which sixties writer and visionary and his band of Merry Pranksters was the book, *The Electric Kool-Aid Test*, about?

4. Who designed the legendary pop art album cover for *Sergeant Pepper's Lonely Hearts Club Band*?

5. Which playwright wrote *Plaza Suite* and *Barefoot in the Park*?

6. Which of the following was not an underground magazine of the 1960s: *Oz, Gandalf's Garden, Nova* or *The International Times*?

7. Who played Professor Higgins in the first stage version of *My Fair Lady*?

8. Who out of the following were not pictured on the cover of *Sergeant Pepper*: Diana Dors, Ghandi, Marilyn Monroe, Marlon Brando or Harold Wilson?

9. Who starred in *Hello Dolly* when the musical opened on Broadway in 1964?

10. What was the name of the London comedy club owned and run by Peter Cook?

11. What fruit featured on the front of an Andy Warhol-designed Velvet Underground album cover?

12. Which French philosopher refused a Nobel Prize in 1954?

13. What Desmond Morris book about human behaviour became a massive bestseller in the late 1960s?

14. Which British literary prize was first established in 1969 and won by PH Newby?

15. Can you name the author of the sixties books: *The Presidential Papers*, *Why Are We in Vietnam?*, and *Cannibals and Christians*?

16. Which Beat poet, and writer of such books as *On the Road*, died in 1969?

17. Whose contribution to Pop Art was blown-up frames of comic strips?

18. Which authoress wrote the *Valley of the Dolls*?

19. Which children's author wrote the screenplay for the Bond film *You Only Live Twice*?

20. Which American novelist wrote *Catch-22*?

21. Which British novelist's first book, *The Collector*, was a critical success in 1963?

22. Which 1961 film, based on a musical, featured two rival gangs, the Sharks and the Jets?

23. Which one of the following satirical magazines was funded by Peter Cook: *Oz, Private Eye* or *Punch*?

24. Architect Sir Basil Spence designed which modern cathedral?

25. Did Philip Roth, Philip Larkin, John Fowles or Tom Robbins write *Portnoy's Complaint*?

26. Which Liverpudlian poet was one of the Liverpool Beat poets and a member of the Scaffold pop group?

27. Gavin Maxwell wrote which popular trilogy about otters during the 1960s?

28. Who wrote *Slaughterhouse 5*?

29. Whose book about his ocean journey on the Kon-Tiki reed raft was published in 1969?

30. Which playwright wrote *Loot* and *What the Butler Saw*, before dying in 1967?

31. *Half a Sixpence* starred Tommy Steele, Cliff Richard or Julie Andrews in the lead role?

32. The musical, *Stop the World – I Want To Get Off*, was co-written by and starred which actor?

33. Which of these three Roald Dahl children's books was the first to be published in the 1960s: *Fantastic Mr Fox*, *James and the Giant Peach* or *Charlie and the Chocolate Factory*?

34. Which author wrote *To Kill a Mockingbird* and won a Pulitzer Prize in 1961?

35. Which Lionel Bart musical, based on a Dickens novel, was Musical of the Year in 1961?

36. Topol became a star after performing in which 1967 musical?

37. Which author wrote *A Burnt-Out Case* and *The Comedians* during the sixties?

38. Which 1968 musical featured the songs *Aquarius, Walking in Space* and *Abie Baby*?

39. *Siddhartha* and *Steppenwolf* were two influential books of the sixties written in the 1920s by which German author?

40. What is the title of Ken Kesey's novel about patients in an Oregon mental hospital?

41. Who wrote *The Electric Kool-Aid Test, The Pump House Gang* and *The Kandy-Kolored Tangerine Flake Streamlined Baby* during the sixties?

42. Anthony Burgess's 1963 novel about a violent future world became essential reading for many in the 1960s. What was the book called?

43. Which infamous book about drug experiences by William S. Burroughs was first published in 1959 but banned in parts of the US until the mid-1960s?

44. Who created the seven hour long experimental film *The Chelsea Girls* in 1966 and *Lonesome Cowboys* three years later?

45. Which British artist produced *A Bigger Splash*, one of many paintings featuring a swimming pool?

46. What was the title of Maurice Sendak's 1963 children's book about a boy called Max, facing up to his childhood fears?

47. Which of the following was not a J. G. Ballard book published in the 1960s: *The Polar World*, *The Drought*, *Crash* or *The Wind from Nowhere*?

48. Which musical featured Harry Secombe in the title role: *Oliver!*, *Pickwick*, *The Boyfriend* or *Our Man Crichton*?

49. Which poet and authoress of *The Bell Jar* committed suicide in 1963?

50. Which influential British poet was she married to?

Sport

1. Who hit six sixes In one cricket over in 1968: Geoffrey Boycott, Dennis Lillee, Gary Sobers or Barry Richards?

2. What was the name of the 1966 World Cup mascot?

3. At which Olympics did Cassius Clay win a boxing medal?

4. Against which team did England begin the 1966 World Cup with a 0-0 draw?

5. How many goals were scored in the famous 1960 European Cup final held at Hampden Park?

6. Was the official attendance at the above game: 135,000, 102,000, 86,000, 72,000 or 68,000?

7. What was the nationality of the Tour de France cycling star Eddie Merckx?

8. Which Australian tennis player won the tennis grand slam for the first time in 1969?

9. Jim Hines, Armin Harry or Tommy Smith was the first sprinter to run the 100 metres in under ten seconds?

10. Mary Rand, Mary Peters or Dorothy Hyman broke the world long jump record in winning Olympic gold in 1964?

11. Which boxer did Cassius Clay beat to become World Heavyweight Champion?

12. Which football team was the first to 'do the double' (win the English League Championship and the FA Cup) in the 20th century?

13. The first ever American Football Superbowl was held in 1967. Did the LA Raiders, Green Bay Packers or the Miami Dolphins win?

14. Which third division London football team created a sensation by winning the 1967 League Cup Final beating first division West Bromwich Albion?

15. Which England wicketkeeper took seven catches In his first Test Match: Godfrey Evans, Alan Knott or Paul Downton?

16. Which continent first hosted the Summer Olympics in 1964?

17. Which Scottish racing driver was killed in a Formula Two race at Hockenheim, Germany, in 1968?

18. Can you name the show jumper who won the 1960 BBC Sports Personality of the Year?

19. Which sports commentator provided the memorable 'They think it's all over' commentary during the 1966 World Cup final?

20. Which fly-half played rugby union for Llanelli, Cardiff and Wales, and was nicknamed 'King'?

21. Which British racing driver won 16 Grand Prix races but never the World Championship title?

22. Which British female swimmer won one of Britain's two gold medals at the 1960s Olympic games, and carried the flag for the British Olympic team at the 1964 games?

23. In which country were the 1968 Summer Olympic games held?

24. Which sporting event was first televised in March 1960?

25. Which American male athlete shattered the world long jump record at the 1968 Olympics?

26. Which bowler was hit for six sixes in one over in 1968?

27. Which one of the following footballers did not play in the 1966 World Cup final win over Germany: Hurst, Greaves, Cohen or Peters?

28. Who partnered Bobby Moore in central defence on the England 1966 World Cup winning team?

29. Which cyclist won BBC Sports Personality of the Year in 1965 only to die on the Tour de France two years later?

30. Which country won the 1962 football World Cup?

31. Who finished above second-place Manchester United to win the 1967-68 English League Championship?

32. Which cricketing captain of England beat the West Indies on tour and in 1968 obtained his 100th cap?

33. Which Portuguese footballer was known as 'the Black Pearl'?

34. Who became the youngest ever Grand Prix World Champion in 1963: Jochen Rindt, Jim Clark or Graham Hill?

35. Who revolutionised high jumping in the late 1960s with his 'flop' technique?

36. 'Henry's Ammer' was a punch thrown by which popular boxer?

37. Which two countries contested the third place play-off at the 1966 World Cup football finals?

38. Who was the captain of Argentina, sent-off in the 1966 World Cup game versus England?

39. Which Asian football team won many hearts at the 1966 World Cup, particularly for their thrilling 5-3 loss to Portugal?

40. What stage did the England football team reach at the 1968 European Championships?

41. Who was in goal for England during their 1966 World Cup football triumph?

42. Who famously batted with a broken arm for England against the West Indies in 1963?

43. Name three of the football teams who played in the Home Internationals, held annually.

44. Henry Cooper fought Muhammad Ali in 1966 at which British football ground?

45. Manchester United's famous late sixties forward line contained an Englishman, an Irishman and a Scotsman. Can you name the Scotsman?

46. Which rugby team's tour of Britain attracted large protests?

47. Which Midlands football team recorded the largest winning margin of a FA Cup final of the 1960s?

48. Which hurdler became the 1968 BBC Sports Personality of the Year?

49. Which of the following teams did England beat at the 1966 World Cup: France, Italy, Argentina, Spain or Portugal?

50. Which football team won the FA Cup three times throughout the 1960s?

films and film stars

1. Which Bond girl emerged from the sea in a bikini as Honey Ryder?

2. Which British actress played the title role in the epic film, *Cleopatra*?

3. Which of the following was not a Cliff Richard film of the 1960s: *Take Me High*, *Wonderful Life*, *Summer Holiday* or *Two A Penny*?

4. Which actor appeared on film as Police Detective Virgil Tibbs?

5. Which one of the following did not appear in *Casino Royale*: David Niven, Deborah Kerr, Orson Welles, Peter Sellers, Ursula Andress, Richard Burton or Woody Allen?

6. Which film of a Neil Simon play, teamed Walther Matthau and Jack Lemmon for the second time?

7. Which children's film starred a flying car alongside Dick Van Dyke and Lionel Jeffries?

8. What was the title of the first Bond film?

9. Which film featured Peter Sellers playing three roles including a mad doctor in a wheelchair?

10. What was the title of the Beatles' second film?

11. Which British singer and his backing band appeared in the 1966 *Thunderbirds are Go* film in puppet form?

12. Which 1960 Oscar-winning film starred Charlton Heston and Yul Brynner?

13. Which memorable screen villain had a white cat as a pet?

14. What film were you watching if you saw cartoon 'Blue Meanies'?

15. Which *Carry On* film was a spoof of the Hammer horror films and featured Oddbod and Oddbod Junior?

16. Who was the 'Cooler King' in *The Great Escape*?

17. What were the names of the three tunnels dug in *The Great Escape*?

18. HAL was a computerised star of which science fiction film?

19. What was the first name of Mrs Robinson's daughter in *The Graduate*: Jackie, Elaine, Jennifer or Paula?

20. Which 1967 film brought us Bagheera and Shere Khan?

21. Joe Buck and Ratzo Rizzo were the leading characters in which 1969 film about hustlers?

22. *How I Learned to Stop Worrying and Love the Bomb* was the alternative title of which 1964 black comedy?

23. Which brutal film of 1920s gangsters starred Faye Dunaway and Warren Beatty?

24. What was the first Bond film to feature Oddjob, an evil henchman?

25. Which South American country do *Butch Cassidy and the Sundance Kid* head to in the 1969 film?

26. Which actor starred as Cool Hand Luke?

27. What was the name of the lead character in *True Grit* played by John Wayne?

28. Pongo and Perdita were starring characters in which 1961 Disney film?

29. Which *Carry On* film starred Kenneth Williams as Julius Caesar and Sid James as Mark Anthony?

30. Sam Bowden's life becomes a nightmare after Max Cady re-enters his life in which 1962 movie?

31. *Springtime for Hitler and Germany* was a 'highlight' of which Mel Brooks film?

32. Which 1969 film first introduced Herbie, a car with a mind of its own?

33. Which film tells the tale of the chaotic search for stolen loot hidden under a Big W sign, featuring Spencer Tracy, Phil Silvers and Mickey Rooney?

34. Which late sixties film featured 'Born to be Wild' by Steppenwolf in its soundtrack?

35. Which 1969 film starred Michael Caine and a fleet of Mini cars?

36. Which *Carry On* film featured the Burpas and the 3rd Foot and Mouth Regiment?

37. Which British crime comedy starred Peter Sellers as Dodger Lane, and Lionel Jeffries as Prison Officer Crout: *No Way Out, Stir Crazy, Two Way Stretch* or *Jail Break*?

38. Which 1960s film ends with Charlton Heston discovering part of the Statue of Liberty?

39. Which one of the following actors did not star in the *Magnificent Seven*: Yul Bryner, James Coburn, Robert Vaughan, James Garner or Steve McQueen?

40. Which film featured the adventures of Jane and Michael Banks and their new nanny?

41. Which 1965 film featured the von Trapp family?

42. How many puppies were found at Cruella De Vil's mansion in *101 Dalmations*: 48, 84, 99 or 101?

43. Holly Golightly was the lead character in which romantic comedy set in New York?

44. Which 1966 film introduced Clint Eastwood as 'the man with no name'?

45. Which 1965 film starred Michael Caine as spy, Harry Palmer?

46. Which was the first James Bond film not to feature Sean Connery in the lead role?

47. Which of the following was not a film starring Elvis Presley: *Blue Hawaii, Wild in the Country, Don't Look Back* or *Kid Galahad*?

48. What was the title of *The Man from U. N. C. L. E.* feature film: *To Trap a Spy or Agents*?

49. What was the name of the 'King of the Swingers' in *The Jungle Book*?

50. Which 1960 film told the tale of a slave played by Kirk Douglas forced to fight as a gladiator?

Advertising and newspapers

1. Which flour brand started using little black and white men in their adverts in the 1960s?

2. In 1964, the *Daily Herald* was transformed into which newspaper still around today?

3. 'Just Flick to Kick' was the advertising slogan of which football game?

4. What sort of creature maintained Cresta soft drinks were 'frothy, man!'?

5. Digby was the first in a line of old English sheepdogs which advertised what product?

6. The powdered potato product, Pom, was renamed in 1967. What was it then advertised as?

7. What sort of bread used balloons in TV advertising to get across its lightness?

8. 'Hands that do dishes' was the slogan of which washing-up product?

9. What sort of fruit was being unzipped on posters in the early 1960s?

10. 'It's fun to build this comical wonder, but woe to the mouse who gets caught under' was the slogan for which popular sixties board game?

11. TV commercials for what sort of product were banned from 1965 onwards?

12. Which British national newspaper was the first to launch a colour supplement?

13. Which Sunday newspaper, previously known as the *Sunday Pictorial,* vied with the *People* as Britain's biggest-selling newspaper: the *Sunday Mirror,* the *News of the World* or the *Sunday Herald*?

14. Cartoons of which pop group were used to launch Nestle's Jellimallo bar in 1963?

15. Which band provided backing music for a cartoon parody of *Juke Box Jury* to advertise Rice Krispies: the Beatles, the Rolling Stones or Genesis?

16. 'A swinging way to start the day' was the advertising slogan for which breakfast cereal?

17. Which toothpaste claimed it offered a 'ring of confidence' from 1967 onwards?

18. Which drink claimed you would 'sleep sweeter' if you drank it before bedtime?

19. Which petrol company urged people to 'put a tiger in their tank'?

20. If 'you've got to grin to get it in', what chocolate snack would you be eating?

21. 'Drinka Pinta - Quencha Thirst' was an advertising slogan for which sort of drink: milk, Tetley's beer or R. Whites lemonade?

22. Which coffee maintained it was 'good to the last drop'?

23. Cadbury's started their long-running and memorable man-in-black advertising campaign in 1968, but for which chocolate?

24. Who was the lead character of the Homepride flour graders: Fred, Ernie, Reg or Paul?

25. Bing Crosby crooned his way through TV adverts for which British petrol station company?

26. Mary Quant's designs extended to an electric oven covered in floral print advertised in the mid-sixties: true or false?

27. The first British TV commercial in colour occurred in 1969 but was it for Bird's Eye peas, Camp coffee or Double Diamond lager?

28. Did the commercial take place in the break of an episode of *Get Smart*, *Thunderbirds*, *The Avengers* or *This Is Your Life*?

29. What chocolate snack was 'full of eastern promise'?

30. Which man accompanied Henry the Bloodhound in advertising dog food?

31. Which car was launched at the start of the decade when it was called an Austin Seven?

32. Which newspaper closed in 1960 after merging with the *Daily Mail*?

33. What sweet was 'made to make your mouth water'?

34. In 1968, which item of underwear made by Gossard was launched?

35. Before cigarette advertising was banned on TV, you were 'never alone' if you had which cigarette brand?

36. Ekco were a popular brand of television sets, mopeds, denim clothes or crockery in the sixties?

37. 'You can taste the trouble they take' was the slogan of which brand of fish finger in the mid-sixties?

38. What child's doll was advertised as the 'the doll you love to dress'?

39. William Franklin uttering 'shhhh' advertised which manufacturer's soft drinks in the sixties?

40. According to sixties adverts, 'things go better with' which soft drink?

41. 'A luxury you can afford by Cyril Lord' referred to what household item?

42. 'Wotalotlgot!' was an advertising slogan for which sweet in the sixties?

43. Which newspaper frequently published comic strips of James Bond throughout the 1960s?

44. What sort of entertainment item was made and advertised by Dansette?

45. Spillers pet foods used a cat to advertise its products but what was its name?

46. Which soap made the user 'a little lovelier each day'?

47. What cleaning product brought back the smile to a pan?

48. Which Sunday newspaper made its first appearance in 1962: the *News of the World*, the *Sunday Telegraph* or the *Observer*?

49. Which credit card was launched in Britain for the first time in 1963?

50. The King Cornet from Lyons Maid was advertised on TV by which British comedian?

Television

1. Which wheelchair-bound detective first hit the screens in the late sixties?

2. 'We're all doomed' and 'Stupid Boy' were catchphrases in which popular British sitcom?

3. What was Tony Hancock's middle name in *Hancock's Half Hour*?

4. Which comedy show, similar to *At Last the 1948 Show*, featured three of the eventual *Monty Python* team along with David Jason?

5. Which American show featured a female genie released from a bottle?

6. Which actor starred as Tony Nelson in the above show?

7. Which American sci-fi show featured the B9 robot and the space family Robinson?

8. The Big Rat gave which puppet boy amazing powers?

9. 'I am not a number – I'm a free man!' was the statement of the lead character in which drama?

10. *Nixon at Nine Five* and *Now for Nixon* were magic shows, music shows or current affairs shows?

11. What was the name of the European version of *It's a Knockout* which first aired in 1967?

12. Which country would you see competing in the above show if the contestants had CH on their outfits?

13. Thora Hird starred in which one of the following BBC sixties sitcoms: *Meet the Wife*, *Nearest and Dearest* and *The Rag Trade*?

14. *No, That's Me Over Here*, was a sitcom written by Barry Cryer, Eric Idle and Graham Chapman as a vehicle for which pint-sized comedian?

15. *Do Not Adjust Your Set* featured which zany music band as its resident musicians?

16. What was the surname of the Air Raid Warden in *Dad's Army*?

17. Patrick Glover's quiet life as a writer is disrupted by his ex-wife, daughters and others, in which show: *Not in Front of the Children*; *Father, Dear Father*; *Man in a Suitcase* or *Sanctuary*?

18. Which rugby league TV commentator became famous for the phrase 'up and under'?

19. Cliff Michelmore hosted which travelogue programme which first appeared on the BBC in 1969?

20. Which show featured the girl-mad medical students of St Swithins?

21. Which influential comedy show featured Carol Cleveland as its single female member of the cast, and made its debut in 1969?

22. Stan Butler's life was plagued by Inspector Blake in which popular sitcom?

23. Which Dr Who frequently played a recorder and was a master of disguise?

24. *Rowan and Martin's Laugh-in* featured: Diane Keaton, Twiggy, Goldie Horn or Natalie Wood as the 'sock it to me girl'?

25. Was the horse in *Steptoe and Son* called Hercules, Champion, Trigger or Dasher?

26. Deryck Guyler played Corky the policeman in which BBC sitcom?

27. *The Troouble Shooters*, featuring characters Stead and Izzard, was about a troubled car manufacturers, oil company, airline or bank?

28. What number was the Prisoner in the show of the same name?

29. Amy Turtle was a leading character in which soap opera?

30. *Lady Don't Fall Backwards* was a novel missing its last page causing which classic sitcom character to embark on a quest?

31. 'Oh, you are awful, but I like you' was a catchphrase of a character in which comedian's show?

32. Time and Relative Dimension in Space was a travelling machine better known by what shortened name?

33. The American action show, *I-Spy*, featured which black American comedian as a secret agent?

34. Which one of the following *Star Trek* characters was not found in the first series: Sulu, Uhura, Chekov or McCoy?

35. Throughout the 1960s, which show was the biggest ratings puller of the year six years out of ten: *The Saint*, *The Royal Variety Performance* or *Saturday Night at the Palladium*?

36. Steve McGarrett headed a crime team on what American island group?

37. Gomez and Morticia were parents in which American show?

38. Stuart Hall was the anchorman on *It's a Knockout* but was the referee: Eddie Waring, Arthur Ellis, Sean Daventry or Christopher Truman?

39. Who referred to his wife as 'a silly moo' and his son-in-law as a 'Scouse git'?

40. Which character comedy show featured Camp Clarence, Kitchener Lampwick and Bovver Boy?

41. Did *Steptoe and Son*, *That Was the Week that Was* or *The Morecambe and Wise Show* gain the largest television audience of the year in 1964?

42. On whose 1963 comedy show did the Beatles appear, only for Ringo to be repeatedly called Bongo?

43. Which show saw Jim Phelps lead the IMF team to solve difficult tasks?

44. What was the name of Samantha's mother in the US show, *Bewitched*?

45. Who wrote and starred in the *Q5* show which first aired in 1969?

46. Who launched their viewers' association to clean-up television during the 1960s?

47. Scientists Tony Newman and Doug Phillips built a top-secret machine to send people into the past or future in which show?

48. David Jason played Captain Fantastic fighting his arch-enemy, Mrs Black, in which of the following shows: *At Last the 1948 Show*, *Do Not Adjust Your Set* or *BBC 3*?

49. What rural soap opera was set in the town of Angleton and was shown on Tuesdays and Thursdays: *The Arrivals*, *Town and Country*, or *The Newcomers*?

50. What family was the focus of the above show?

Events

1. Who became India's first female Prime Minister in 1966?

2. Who was the second man on the moon?

3. In which year was the first Christmas stamp produced by the GPO?

4. What was the name of the call girl at the centre of the 1963 Profumo scandal?

5. Can you name the blonde-haired model involved in the above episode?

6. Which country did Golda Maier become leader of in 1969?

7. In what year was the Woodstock Free Festival of Art and Music?

8. In which US city was President John F. Kennedy assassinated?

9. What was the name of the dog who found the football World Cup trophy in a South London garden in March 1966?

10. In 1960, which Asian country became led by the world's first female Prime Minister?

11. Who became leader of the Labour Party in 1963?

12. Who, along with Myra Hindley, was found guilty of the Moors murders in 1966?

13. Which Eastern European country did the USSR invade in 1968?

14. Which member of the royal family was born in 1960?

15. Can you name either of the two American athletes who raised their fist in a black power salute on the Olympic podium in 1968?

16. And what event had they won Olympic medals in: the 100 metres, the 200 metres or the 800 metres?

17. Which British bridge was sold to an American oil company in 1968?

18. What was the name of the first successful communications satellite: Telstar, Comsat 1 or Echo 1?

19. The novel, *Lady Chatterley's Lover*, was the subject of a court case in 1960 but who was the author?

20. Who completed his solo round the world yacht voyage in May 1967?

21. Which Russian ballet dancer defected to the West in 1961?

22. Which Mediterranean island became independent of Britain in 1961?

23. In which year did Britain launch its first space satellite, Ariel 1: 1962, 1965 or 1968?

24. What type of public transport disappeared from London by the end of 1962?

25. Which satellite made live TV possible across the Atlantic for the first time in 1962?

26. An agreement to build a supersonic airliner was signed in 1962 by Britain and which other nation?

27. Who, in 1965, became the first footballer to receive a knighthood?

28. What covered London in December 1962, causing more than 50 deaths?

29. Which French President spoke out against Britain's attempts to join the Common Market in 1962?

30. The Beeching report was about Britain's trade unions, railways, motorway system or captial punishment?

31. Which spacecraft took photos of Mars in 1964: Cosmos 8, Voyager 3, Mariner 4 or Moskhod 2?

32. Who was known as Viscount Stansgate before he renounced his title in 1963?

33. A telephone hotline was set up between the two Superpowers in 1963. It ran between the White House and which other building?

34. Who resigned in 1963 to be replaced by Sir Alec Douglas-Home?

35. Which television station began broadcasting in 1964?

36. Which member of the royal family was born in 1964?

37. In what month of 1963 was President Kennedy assassinated?

38. Did the USSR, China or the US perform the first docking of two spacecraft in 1967?

39. Who was sentenced to life imprisonment in South Africa in 1964 for his fight against apartheid?

40. Who became the leader of the Soviet Union in October 1964: Kruschev, Brezhnev, Andropov or Stenislav?

41. Which African leader declared a Unilateral Declaration of Independence (UDI) in 1965?

42. Who became leader of the Conservative Party in 1965?

43. Ranger 7 took the first close-up photos of what object in 1964?

44. What district of San Francisco saw the pioneering development of the Hippie movement?

45. Which African country was led by President Jomo Kenyatta from 1964?

46. Herman Titov, Valentina Tereshkova or Leonid Brezan was the second Russian in space?

47. In 1960, the Archbishop of Canterbury held talks for the first time in 500 years with which religious figure?

48. In which country was the Tet Offensive held?

49. In 1965, Elizabeth Lane became Britain's first female surgeon, High Court Judge, police chief or football referee?

50. In April 1963, 70,000 marchers began a demonstration from Aldermaston, London. What were they demonstrating against?

Music

1. Who was the very first disc jockey on BBC Radio One?

2. And what was the first song that he played?

3. 'Itchycoo Park' and 'Lazy Sunday' were hits for which popular mod outfit?

4. Which artist's brainchild was 'The Exploding Plastic Inevitable', an experimental late sixties performance?

5. Which soul singer had a huge hit with the song 'When a Man Loves a Woman'?

6. Which seminal late sixties band featured Grace Slick as a songwriter and singer?

7. Which soul singer first came to prominence at age 13 with the record, 'Fingertips'?

8. 'Runaround Sue' was a 1961 hit for: Dion, Adam Faith or Georgie Fame?

9. Which group did Diana Ross leave in 1969?

10. 'The Carnival is Over' was a hit for: the Drifters, the Seekers, the Turtles or the Sonics?

11. Which two of the following acts did not play at Altamont Speedway in 1969 along with the Rolling Stones: Santana, King Crimson, the Flying Burrito Brothers or Canned Heat?

12. Which island hosted a major musical festival in both 1968 and 1969?

13. Which band's debut album was *Music from Big Pink*: the Yardbirds, Them, the Band or the Byrds?

14. 'Dancing in the Street' was a hit for which Motown records female group?

15. Alan Price had a novelty hit with a Randy Newman song about Simon Smith and what sort of bear?

16. Manfred Mann had a hit with 'Mighty Quinn', but who wrote the song: Jopan Baez, Bob Dylan, Joni Mitchell or John Lennon?

17. Which female singer had hits with 'Son of a Preacher Man' and 'I Only Want to be With You'?

18. 'Out of Time' was a number one hit for Chris Farlowe and the Thunderbirds but was it written by Lennon and McCartney, Jagger and Richards or Bob Dylan?

19. Which Beatles song knocked 'A Whiter Shade of Pale' off the number one spot in the summer of 1967?

20. Who replaced Steve Marriot as lead singer of the Small Faces: Rod Stewart, Eric Clapton or Ronnie Wood?

21. Who was the producer of songs as varied as 'Instant Karma' by John Lennon and 'You've Lost That Lovin' Feeling' by the Righteous Brothers?

22. Can you name the two Monkees hit singles which featured the word 'Believer' in their titles?

23. Who sang 'Sunshine Superman' in 1966?

24. Which seriously psychedelic band had albums including *Incense and Peppermints, The World in a Seashell* and *Good Morning Starshine*?

25. Which was the first Beatles single featuring an A side song written by George Harrison?

26. *The Piper at the Gates of Dawn* was the first album from which band?

27. 'Heroin' and 'Venus in Furs' were songs found on what 1967 album?

28. 'Sugar, Sugar' was a 1969 hit for which 'bubblegum' pop band?

29. Buffalo Springfield featured which two members of Crosby, Stills, Nash and Young?

30. Which Hendrix album cover caused a furore with its large number of naked women?

31. Which Rolling Stones album was the first to feature the songs 'The Last Time' and 'Satisfaction'?

32. 'My Girl' was a major hit for which soul group?

33. Steve Winwood was in which of the following sixties groups: the Turtles, Blind Faith, the Spencer Davies Group, the Zombies or Traffic?

34. Genesis recorded their first album in early 1969. What was it called?

35. Who was the first Beatle to release a solo album in the UK?

36. 'All the Time in the World' was the theme song for which Bond movie?

37. Who sang the above song for the film?

38. Which rock 'n' roll singer was backed by the Tornados from 1963 onwards: Joe Brown, Adam Faith, Billy Fury or Eddie Cochrane?

39. In what year did the Beatles play their last UK tour?

40. 'White Rabbit' and 'Somebody to Love' were hit singles for which psychedelic late sixties band?

41. Which two of the following acts were signed to the Beatles' Apple Records label: Badfinger, Dusty Springfield, the Soft Parade, Mary Hopkin or the Incredible String Band?

42. *Get The Picture?*, *Emotions* and *SF Sorrow* were albums by which English rock band?

43. Otis Redding died in a plane crash. What song of his was released in the aftermath of his death and became a huge hit?

44. 'Don't Look Back' was a documentary film looking at which sixties artist?

45. 'Aquarius' was a 1969 hit for: Spirit, 5th Dimension, the Incredible String Band or Donovan?

46. Which song spent more weeks at number one in Britain in 1967: 'All You Need is Love', 'The Last Waltz', 'I'm a Believer' or 'A Whiter Shade of Pale'?

47. Who was one of four joint winners of the 1969 Eurovision Song Contest with 'Boom-Bang-a-Bang'?

48. Which Australian artist, better known as a TV presenter today, occupied the number one spot in the charts as the sixties ended and the seventies began?

49. 'Louie Louie' was a hit for the Moody Blues, the Kingsmen, the Move or the Nice?

50. The instrumental hit, 'Telstar', was performed by the Tornados, the Shadows, the Surfaris or the Mar-Kays?

Sport

1. Which American boxer was stripped of his world title after refusing the draft to fight in Vietnam?

2. Which golfer became known as the Golden Bear?

3. In what year did Manchester United win the European Cup final?

4. Which Yorkshire fast bowler took 132 wickets in the 1960 season?

5. Who was the only boxer to win the BBC Sports Personality of the Year award throughout the 1960s?

6. What was the name of the only England manager to lift the World Cup?

7. Who scored a hat-trick for Real Madrid in the 1960 European Cup final?

8. Who became the first British woman to win an athletics gold at the Olympics?

9. Which English footballer scored a staggering 44 goals in only 57 games for his country?

10. Which tennis player won the Wimbledon Ladies Singles in 1966, 1967 and 1968?

11. In 1962, Wilt Chamberlain broke US basketball records by scoring 55, 65, 80 or 100 points in a single game?

12. In the 1968 Olympics, Kenyan runner Kip Keino won the 1,500 metres, came second in the 5,000 metres but collapsed in which event?

13. What was the name of the Soviet Union's goalkeeper nicknamed the 'Black Panther'?

14. Which English county won cricket's County Championship for the very first time in 1961?

15. Who was the England football manager before Sir Alf Ramsey: Walter Winterbottom, Don Revie, Matt Busby or Jack Hanson?

16. Which British driver won the 1963 Grand Prix Championship: Jim Clark, Graham Hill or Jackie Stewart?

17. Who won the English 1961-1962 Football League Championship: Burnley, Manchester United, Ipswich Town or Liverpool?

18. Which female American sprinter won three gold medals at the 1960 Olympics?

19. In which round of their first fight did Henry Cooper floor Cassius Clay?

20. Which was the first English team to appear in the final of a European competition in the 1960s: Arsenal, Birmingham City, Manchester United or Aston Villa?

21. What was the final score after extra time in the 1966 World Cup final held at Wembley Stadium?

22. In what year did the first Cooper versus Clay fight occur?

23. Which club was the first English winner of a European trophy in the 1960s: Tottenham Hotspur, Wolverhampton Wanderers, Manchester City or Arsenal?

24. Which national rugby union side featured sixties legends such as Ken Gray, Kel Tremain and Colin Meads?

25. Who became World Heavyweight Boxing Champion in 1962: Henry Cooper, Sonny Liston, Cassius Clay or Brian London?

26. In what year were substitutes allowed in English football matches for the first time?

27. Who, in 1965, finally retired from professional football at the age of fifty?

28. Which county won the County Cricket Championship in 1966: Surrey, Yorkshire, Lancashire or Sussex?

29. Which London football team won the European Cup Winners' Cup in 1965?

30. At which sport did American, Willie Shoemaker excel in the 1960s?

31. Which wicketkeeper made his debut for England in 1967?

32. Which football team won the FA Cup twice during the 1960s?

33. Which US basketball team were professional champions every year between 1960 and 1966?

34. Which Scottish club won the European Cup in 1967?

35. How many times did Rod Laver win Wimbledon throughout the sixties?

36. For which side did fast bowler Wes Hall terrorise English and other batsman during the 1960s?

37. Which English footballer moved from Milan to Spurs in 1961?

38. Which country dominated the Davis Cup tennis competition, winning seven titles during the 1960s?

39. Who scored 310 runs for England against New Zealand in 1965?

40. Who was manager of Manchester United throughout the 1960s?

41. The England cricket team met Australia for the 50th, 100th or 200th time during 1968?

42. In what year was the Football League Cup introduced?

43. Which team left the English football league in 1962: Barrow, Wycombe Wanderers, Accrington Stanley or Aldershot?

44. Oxford United, Cambridge United or Southend United entered the English football league in 1962?

45. Who took his 300th Test wicket in 1964: Fred Truman, Derek Underwood or Wes Hall?

46. What nationality was golfer Gary Player?

47. Which West Indian all-rounder played 86 consecutive Test Matches from the late fifties right through the sixties?

48. In which country were the 1962 World Cup Football finals held?

49. Who conceded Tony Jacklin's putt in the 1969 Ryder Cup, which ensured that the entire competition was a draw?

50. What was the name of the sole 1969 FA Cup final scorer, a name shared with a member of sixties band Buffalo Springfield?

Science and Technology

1. Who was the first man in space: John Glenn, Neil Armstrong or Yuri Gagarin?

2. By what name did the drug Diazepan become better known during the sixties?

3. Who became the first American astronaut to orbit the earth in a spacecraft?

4. Who performed the first human heart transplant in 1967?

5. Which Apollo mission was the first to place men in an orbit around the moon?

6. Rachel Carson's 1963 book warned of the potential effects of introducing chemicals into the ecosystem. What was the book called?

7. What was the name of Europe's longest road bridge which opened in the UK in 1964?

8. What building became the highest in Britain when it was officially opened in 1965?

9. When were soft contact lenses invented: 1965, 1969 or 1960?

10. Which company first produced instant colour photographs in 1963?

11. Dolby noise reduction system was invented in: 1960, 1963, 1967 or 1969?

12. Who was the third member of the crew during the first ever moon landings?

13. What large airliner made its maiden flight at the end of the 1960s?

14. What household device became front loading at home for the first time in the 1960s?

15. Which animal became the symbol of the World Wildlife Fund which was formed in 1961?

16. Unimates were the world's first working hovercraft, robots, computers or transistor radios?

17. In 1964, what form of cancer treatment was first used?

18. In 1965, Aleksei Leonov performed the first spacewalk, landed on the moon or flew the first supersonic jet fighter?

19. Douglas Englebart invented what computer device in 1964?

20. In space technology what did LEM stand for?

21. Which doctor, with a *Star Trek* character surname, was an influential expert on how to bring up babies and children in the 1960s?

22. What type of pen was invented in Japan in 1963?

23. Which fruit, previously known as the Chinese gooseberry, was marketed in the 1960s by New Zealand?

24. What sort of USSR military weapon was codenamed Foxbat in the West?

25. What hovered for the first time in 1963: VTOL aircraft, Flymo lawnmowers or helicopters?

26. What type of object in space was discovered by Jocelyn Bell in 1967: meteorites, quarks, pulsars or comets?

27. Shakey was an early example of: a video recorder, a mobile robot, a colour television or a handheld computer?

28. In 1969 what aircraft capable of vertical take off and landing entered service with the RAF?

29. The Nimrod anti-submarine aircraft was developed from which airliner?

30. At the end of the 1960s, which was the fastest aircraft out of the following: Concorde, the SR71 Blackbird, the TU-144 or the Mig 23?

31. Which airline was the first in the world to fly Boeing 747 airliners?

32. What advanced jet fighter project was cancelled by the British government: the F111, the TSR-2 or the FT107?

33. Strong debates about the use of chlorine, fluoride or riboflavin in drinking water occurred during the 1960s?

34. Which country introduced its Bullet Train service in the mid-1960s?

35. Was Luna 1, Mercury 1, Vostok 1 or Gemini 1 the first craft to carry a person into space?

36. Roy Jacuzzi was the 1960s inventor of the spa bath which took his name: true or false?

37. Watson and Crick were awarded a Nobel Prize for work on DNA, heart surgery or superconductivity?

38. What drug, given to pregnant mothers, resulted in hundreds of children born with deformed or missing limbs?

39. What sort of vehicle was the SRN4 Mark 3 which saw service from 1968 onwards?

40. What was the maximum number of passengers the above vehicle could carry: 14, 40 or 400?

41. What was the space rocket launch site in Florida called before it became known as Cape Kennedy?

42. Watches using what type of crystal were developed in the 1960s?

43. What was the name of the oil tanker that caused an environmental disaster when it crashed off the coast of England in 1967?

44. Established in 1969, ARPANET was the forerunner of which essential communications system today?

45. Which Apollo spacecraft was destroyed by fire on the ground, killing three astronauts?

46. Which electronics company introduced the audio cassette in the 1960s?

47. What nationality was surgeon, Christiaan Barnard, who sprung to prominence in the late 1960s?

48. The UK's first motorway service station was opened on which motorway?

49. Dr Denton Cooley performed the first heart transplant, the first liver transplant, the first artificial heart transplant or the first kidney transplant?

50. Luna 9, Apollo 7 or US Surveyor 1 was the first machine to soft land on the surface of the moon?

Kids' Television

1. In what object did Top Cat live?

2. What were the shapes of the three windows in *Play School*?

3. Muskie and Vince assisted which canine law enforcer in a popular sixties cartoon?

4. What was the name of the cow in the *Magic Roundabout*?

5. What colour was Ivor the Engine?

6. Which popular TV puppet show finished being shown on the BBC in 1968, but was later broadcast on ITV?

7. Who is Bamm-Bamm's father: Fred Flintstone or Barney Rubble?

8. Can you name the only two *Magic Roundabout* characters with Mr in front of their names?

9. What sort of creature was *The Herbs* character, Dill?

10. Which western law enforcer was masked and used silver bullets?

11. Of the classic *Blue Peter* line-up comprising Valerie Singleton, Peter Purves and John Noakes, which of the three joined the show last?

12. What was the name of the chimpanzee in *Daktari*: Clarence, Judy, JT or Hedley?

13. What was the name of Ivor the Engine's driver?

14. What was the name of the gorilla in the *Banana Splits*?

15. Prudence the Kitten had a sister called Petunia, Primrose or Petula?

16. Whose instruction to a collie dog, 'Get Down Shep', became a national catchphrase?

17. What was the name of the lion in the *Huckleberry Hound* show whose catchphrases included 'Heavens to Murgatroyd'?

18. Admiral Harriman Nelson commanded Seaview in which underwater show?

19. Assisted by his sidekick, Gurth, in their fight against King John, Roger Moore played the lead character in what show?

20. Sooty first appeared on TV in 1952 but in 1964 he was joined by which female character?

21. What was the name of the Cabin Boy who frequently saved Captain Pugwash's skin?

22. Steve Zodiac piloted which Gerry Anderson show's spaceship?

23. Dr Mopp was first found in *Chigley*, *Trumpton* or *Camberwick Green*?

24. What was the numberplate of Lady Penelope's Rolls Royce?

25. What was the surname of George, Jane, Judy and Elroy: a futuristic cartoon family?

26. What was the name of Bill and Ben, the Flowerpot Men's tortoise friend: Speedy, Slowcoach, Pacey or Plodder?

27. Who was Captain Pugwash's evil adversary?

28. Who was the eldest of the Tracy brothers who piloted Thunderbird 1?

29. What was the name of the dog and leader of the *Banana Splits*: Beagle, Fleagle or Rover?

30. What was the name of the Lumberjack who raced the Buzz Wagon in *Wacky Races*?

31. Which cartoon show featured a shape changer called Bez who would cry, 'Size of a...'?

32. What popular show gave away special pencils to contestants?

33. The second ever *Blue Peter* appeal in 1964 saw 7.5 tons of silver paper collected, this bought: a lifeboat, three flats for homeless people or two guide dogs for the blind?

34. What was the race number of the car driven by Dick Dastardly in *Wacky Races*?

35. What colour hair did Fred Flintstone's wife, Wilma, have?

36. What sort of creature was Lulu who ran amok memorably in the *Blue Peter* studio?

37. What was the name of the police officer in *Top Cat*?

38. What instrument did Sooty often play?

39. The Merioneth and Llantisilly Rail Traction Company Limited was featured in which animated train show?

40. Which show featured a young Dennis Waterman in the starring role of a naughty schoolboy along with his gang called *The Outlaws*?

41. Pinky, of *Pinky and Perky* fame, wore red, blue or green clothing?

42. Which story-telling show on the BBC often featured Kenneth Williams or Bernard Cribbins and started in 1965?

43. How many teddy bears were there in *Play School*?

44. Which show for the deaf and hard of hearing featured Tony Hart and Wilf Lunn among others?

45. Who were Captain Scarlet's arch-enemies?

46. Which TV show featured a panel of four adults who answered viewer's questions?

47. Sonny Hammond had a great kangaroo friend known by what name?

48. Jack Hargreaves was one of the four presenters of *How?* Can you name one of the others?

49. Can you name the 12 year-old boy or his faithful German Shepard dog in *Champion the Wonder Horse*?

50. Was the Jetsons' dog called Rosie, Astro, Moonbeam or Roger?

Music

1. Which Merseybeat band had a hit with 'How Do You Do It'?

2. Which of the following was not a drummer in a well-known sixties band: Keith Moon, Charlie Watts, Paul Kantner or Mitch Mitchell?

3. The Chiffons had a hit with 'My Sweet Lord', 'She's So Fine', 'She's Not There' or 'Nowhere Man'?

4. How many albums had Led Zeppelin released by the end of the 1960s?

5. Psychedelic rock outfit, Vanilla Fudge's biggest hit was a cover of 'You Keep Me Hanging On', but which group made that song famous first?

6. Whose first two albums were *Song to a Seagull* and *Clouds*?

7. 'Break On Through (To The Other Side)', 'Light My Fire' and 'The End' were all found on the Doors' first, third or fourth album?

8. The Doors took their name from *The Doors of Perception* but who was this book by?

9. 'Rainy Day Women #12 and 35' was the opening track on which classic Dylan album?

10. 'Revolution' and 'Back in the USSR' can be found on which Beatles' long playing record?

11. Which band pioneered garage rock with their *Kick out the Jams* album?

12. What song gave the Beatles their last number one on the Parlophone record label?

13. Who originally hosted *Juke Box Jury*: David Jacobs, Peter Murray, Gilbert Harding or Jimmy Saville?

14. Which one of the following bands did not hail from Liverpool: the Beatles, Gerry and the Pacemakers, the Merseybeats or the Troggs?

15. The Fillmore Auditorium venue played host to acts including Jefferson Airplane, the Grateful Dead and Jimi Hendrix, but in which American city was it located?

16. What famous Dylan song was the first track of the album, *Highway 61 Revisited*?

17. Arthur Lee fronted which band whose most famous album was *Forever Changes*?

18. Moby Grape, the 13th Floor Elevators or Strawberry Alarm Clock were a psychedelic sixties outfit formed by ex-members of Jefferson Airplane?

19. Whose songs included, 'The Wind Cries Mary', 'Castles Made of Sand' and 'If 6 was 9'?

20. Which band had chart success with 'He ain't Heavy, He's My Brother': the Hollies, the Doors, the Tyrelles or the Tremeloes?

21. 'I Can See for Miles' and 'Pictures of Lily' were songs by which British band?

22. The Aces recorded one of the first reggae hits in the UK with which artist?

23. Who was the female singer on the sexually explicit song 'Je t'aime' which was banned by many radio stations?

24. Who was the male singer on the record 'Je t'aime'?

25. How old was Lulu when she had a hit record with 'Shout'?

26. Marianne Faithful's debut single, 'As Tears Go By', was written by the songwriters of which well-known band?

27. The Who were called the Artwoods, the High Numbers or the Who Gives a Damn when they released their first single, 'I'm The Face/Zoot Suit' in 1964?

28. What Beatles EP featured four figures dressed as furry animals on its cover?

29. Which one of the following bands was not part of the Surf scene which hit Britain: Dick Dale, Jan and Dean or the Turtles?

30. Which female singer sang 'Downtown' and 'I Know a Place'?

31. Which 1969 Rolling Stones album featured 'Gimme Shelter' and 'You Can't Always Get What You Want'?

32. The Wildcats backed which early sixties singer?

33. Who was the lead singer of the Animals who later went on to be part of the group, War?

34. Which Liverpool-based music paper started publiction in 1961?

35. Which keyboard player was often referred to as the sixth Rolling Stone: Gary Brooker, Billy Ocean, Ian Stewart or Rick Wakeman?

36. Which song talked of 'sixteen vestal virgins' and featured the keyboards and vocals of Gary Brooker?

37. Which of the following did not play bass guitar in well-known sixties bands: Paul McCartney, John Entwistle, Steve Marriot or Bill Wyman?

38. Did Brian Poole, Paul Anka or Gary Puckett sing with the Union Gap on tracks including 'Lady Willpower', 'Over You' and 'Don't Give in to Him'?

39. The famous Crawdaddy Club, which saw early performances by bands like the Rolling Stones, was based in Richmond, Soho, Croydon or Harlesden?

40. Which two of the following songs appeared on *The Freewheelin'* Bob Dylan album: 'A Hard Rain's a-Gonna Fall', 'Mr Tambourine Man', 'Like a Rolling Stone' or 'Masters of War'?

41. Which of the following bands did not grow up in the 1965-68 San Francisco scene: the Grateful Dead, Country Joe and the Fish, MC5s or Moby Grape?

42. Which band recorded 'Dedicated Follower of Fashion', a song later covered by Petula Clark?

43. *Dragon Fly* was the title of an album by both the Strawbs and which San Francisco-based psychedelic band?

44. 'Walking Back to Happiness' was an early 1960s hit for which schoolgirl singer?

45. Who sang about the 'Leader of the Pack' in 1964?

46. Which Rolling Stones album came first: *Aftermath*, *Beggars Banquet* or *Their Satanic Majesties Request*?

47. Can you complete the name of the following Merseybeat band, Rory Storm...?

48. Which American male singer had an early sixties hit with `I left My Heart in San Francisco'?

49. `Knock on Wood' was a hit for Edwin Starr, Eddie Floyd or Robert Parker?

50. The McCoys, the Turtles or the Lovin's Spoonful had a major success with the song, `Hang on Sloopy'?

Answers

fun and Games

1. Barbie
2. Cluedo
3. Twister
4. Operation
5. Mouse Trap
6. Scalextric
7. KerPlunk
8. Frisbee
9. Tonka
10. Whizzing Willy and Spinning Sammy

11. Etch-a-Sketch
12. Paul
13. Blue
14. Tiny Tears
15. Spirograph
16. Identity tags, equipment manual, training manual
17. Cliff Richard
18. 1/72
19. Monopoly
20. G.I. Joe

21. Five inches
22. Ten shillings
23. The Bat Utility Belt
24. Noddy
25. Sixteen
26. Blue
27. Lego

28. Play Doh
29. Spirograph
30. Jim Clark

31. Mr Potato Head
32. Sea Monkeys
33. 75
34. Eight
35. Red
36. Players were made three-dimensional for the first time
37. Colonel Mustard, Professor Plum and Reverend Green
38. Travel down the wooden staircase
39. Hammer
40. Tiny Tears

41. Yellow
42. Hot Wheels
43. Red
44. False
45. *The Man from U.N.C.L.E.*
46. Six
47. Brain Ache
48. Mrs White, Miss Scarlett and Mrs Peacock
49. Thunderbird 4
50. Orange

QUIZ 2

Music

1. Cilla Black
2. The Grateful Dead
3. Pete Best
4. Genesis and Yes
5. Pink Floyd
6. Jimmy Saville
7. Sandie Shaw
8. Boots ('Kinky Boots')
9. Jimi Hendrix
10. Radio Caroline

11. Eleven
12. Mick Taylor
13. The Searchers
14. Amen Corner
15. Radio Emerald and Radio Jackson
16. George Martin
17. Peter Green
18. True
19. Sandie Shaw
20. *Thunderball*

21. No
22. Lonnie Donegan
23. The Everly Brothers
24. Mike Berry and Peter Tosh
25. Wendy Richards
26. 'Nut Rocker'

27. 'I Want To Hold Your Hand'
28. *Rolling Stone*
29. Peter Noone
30. The Incredible String Band

31. Brian Jones
32. 'It's Not Unusual'
33. Rolf Harris
34. Elvis Presley
35. Janis Joplin
36. Cream
37. Simon and Garfunkel
38. Berry Gordy
39. The Beach Boys
40. Matt Monro

41. 'Subterranean Homesick Blues'
42. *Head*
43. *Revolver*
44. Mary Hopkin
45. Jim Reeves
46. Phil Spector
47. The Lovin's Spoonful or the Mamas and the Papas
48. Radio Caroline
49. Brian Epstein
50. Them

QUIZ 3

Kids' Television

1. *Crackerjack*
2. *The Sooty Show*
3. The Creepy Coupe
4. Pink
5. True
6. Bingo
7. Susan Stranks
8. Windy Miller
9. *Pogle's Wood*
10. Flipper

11. Uncle Oregano
12. Jeff Tracy
13. Johnny Morris
14. 1960
15. Mr Brackett
16. Marina
17. *Tales of the Riverbank*
18. Captain Snort
19. Jemima
20. Troy Tempest

21. Captain Pugwash
22. *Crackerjack*
23. *The Arabian Knights*
24. Parker
25. Petra
26. *Supercar*

27. True
28. Minerva
29. Thunderbird 5
30. *The Woodentops*

31. Looby Loo
32. Commissioner Gordon or Chief O'Hara
33. False
34. *The Singing Ringing Tree*
35. 'Clementine'
36. Mr Jinks
37. *Supercar*
38. *The Flintstones*
39. *The Magic Roundabout*
40. *Champion the Wonder Horse*

41. Christopher Trace
42. The Sour Grapes Gang
43. Gordon
44. Mummy Woodentop
45. A lion
46. *Stingray*
47. A dragon
48. Five
49. *Wacky Races*
50. Brains

QUIZ 4

Fashion

1. Mods
2. Jean Shrimpton
3. Carnaby Street
4. Vidal Sassoon
5. Yves St Laurent
6. Nancy Sinatra
7. Doris Day
8. Mary Quant
9. Culottes
10. Jackie Kennedy

11. Winkle-pickers
12. Chelsea Boots
13. Mary Quant
14. Plastic
15. Nehru Jacket
16. Op Art
17. Love Beads
18. Bis (Dorothée Bis)
19. Ossie Clark
20. Kings Road

21. *The Avengers*
22. Yves St Laurent
23. *Barbarella*
24. London
25. David Bailey

26. Mary Quant
27. Duck's Arse
28. A daisy
29. Shoes
30. Sandals

31. Jackie Kennedy
32. Psychedelic
33. True
34. Vintage Clothing
35. Tights
36. Twiggy
37. The Afghan
38. The Maxi
39. Dr Scholl
40. Cathy McGowan

41. Kipper ties
42. Peter Townsend
43. George Best
44. Men
45. Carnaby Street
46. Fulham
47. A dress
48. Yes
49. Turtleneck sweater
50. Mary Quant

Answers

QUIZ 5

Television

1. *Dad's Army*
2. Bamber Gascoigne
3. *Coronation Street*
4. *Z Cars*
5. Noughts and crosses
6. *Crossroads*
7. *War Games*
8. Bob Monkhouse
9. Bernie the Bolt
10. *Bewitched*

11. The Duke of Edinburgh
12. *Police 5*
13. *The Man from U.N.C.L.E.*
14. Dudley Moore
15. *That Was the Week that Was*
16. The Hollies and the Swinging Blue Jeans
17. Pinky and Perky and the Beatles
18. 1960
19. *University Challenge*
20. *Steptoe and Son*

21. *News at Ten*
22. The USS Enterprise
23. *A for Andromeda*
24. *The Rag Trade*

25. *Sykes*
26. The second
27. *Dr Finlay's Casebook*
28. *Fireball XL5*
29. A consumer affairs programme
30. 1965

31. *It's a Knockout*
32. *People and Places*
33. Saturdays
34. Patrick Troughton
35. *Take a Letter*
36. Shaw Taylor
37. *Peyton Place*
38. Doctor 'Bones' McCoy
39. *That Was the Week that Was*
40. Corporal Jones

41. Private Walker
42. *The Goon Show*
43. *Coronation Street*
44. The Gojos
45. True
46. *H R Pufnstuf*
47. Elsie Grimshaw
48. Curry and Chips
49. Jill and Sandy
50. Hattie Jacques

QUIZ 6

cełebrities

1. Ronnie and Reggie Kray
2. John Profumo
3. Marilyn Monroe
4. John Lennon
5. Martin Luther King
6. Che Guevara
7. David Bailey
8. Edward Heath
9. Ringo Starr
10. The Boston Strangler

11. Mia Farrow
12. Sir Winston Churchill
13. Anita Pallenberg
14. Edward (Ted) Kennedy
15. Robert Kennedy
16. Donald Campbell
17. Lenny Bruce
18. Richard Burton and Elizabeth Taylor
19. George Best
20. Sharon Tate

21. 1965
22. Pablo Picasso
23. 1969
24. Enoch Powell
25. Simon Dee

26. Britt Ekland
27. 1962
28. Dr Timothy Leary
29. David Steel
30. Jane Fonda

31. Andrew Loog Oldham
32. Jackie Kennedy
33. The Animals
34. Barbara Castle
35. James Hanratty
36. Che Guevara
37. Lulu
38. Malcolm X
39. George Harrison
40. Four

41. Gibraltar
42. Peter Cook, Dudley Moore, Alan Bennett and Jonathon Miller
43. Maharishi Mahesh Yogi
44. Tony Hancock
45. Jacqueline Bisset
46. Pattie Boyd
47. The Manson Family
48. Martin Luther King
49. Donald Campbell
50. Joan Baez

QUIZ 7

Events

1. Paris
2. Gary Powers
3. The GPO Tower
4. 1964
5. Hong Kong
6. The Dartford Tunnel
7. Israel
8. Contraception advice for young people
9. Martin Luther King
10. Washington DC

11. Nigeria
12. France
13. 1963
14. Switzerland
15. Jack Ruby
16. George Blake
17. Lyndon Johnson
18. Brighton
19. Muhammad Ali
20. Foot and Mouth Disease

21. Sweden
22. The Great Train Robbery
23. South Africa
24. France

25. 1964
26. Giant Pandas
27. Northern Ireland
28. The Rolling Stones
29. 1968
30. Arkle

31. Florence
32. France
33. Lyndon Johnson
34. True
35. Sam Cooke
36. Seamen
37. Ronan Point
38. Apollo 11
39. 1967
40. Khrushchev

41. Ho Chi Minh
42. Richard Nixon
43. Kim Philby
44. 1968 Mexico Games
45. Rhodesia
46. The Rolling Stones
47. China
48. Berlin
49. 2.6 million pounds
50. Jack Fenshaw

QUIZ 8

Music

1. George Harrison
2. False
3. The Zombies
4. Tony Blackburn
5. The Yardbirds
6. Aretha Franklin
7. Creedence Clearwater Revival
8. Pirate radio stations
9. The Shadows
10. 'Get Back'

11. Billy Ocean (billed as the Beatles with Billy Preston)
12. The Shadows
13. The Surfaris
14. The Jimi Hendrix Experience
15. 'A Day in the Life'
16. Napoleon XIV
17. Cream
18. Joe Meek
19. Ike and Tina Turner
20. The Righteous Brothers

21. True
22. 'I Saw Her Standing There'
23. Englebert Humperdinck
24. Jimi Hendrix

25. John Prine
26. Fairport Convention
27. 1967
28. Herb Alpert
29. *Top of the Pops*
30. Sonny and Cher

31. Gary Puckett and the Union Gap
32. Ben E. King
33. Elvis Presley
34. *Ready, Steady, Go*
35. Hyde Park, London
36. The Marvelettes
37. 'Eight Miles High'
38. The Band
39. Bass guitar
40. Jeff Banks

41. The Yardbirds
42. Frank Zappa
43. *Beatles for Sale*
44. The Marquee Club
45. The Mothers of Invention
46. The Twist
47. The Small Faces
48. And the Dakotas
49. The Spencer Davies Group
50. James Brown

QUIZ 9

Life

1. Radio Luxembourg
2. 12
3. Victoria
4. Milk at break times
5. Billy Whizz
6. Betting shops
7. Panda crossings
8. The 50 pence piece
9. *Misty*
10. New Towns

11. Green Shield Stamps
12. 70mph
13. TV Tornado
14. Janet and John
15. V.A.T.
16. Eggs
17. Minnie the Minx
18. 20
19. Milton Keynes
20. First and second class stamps

21. The Greater London Council
22. *The Eagle*
23. 21
24. 1960

25. Radio One
26. Parking tickets
27. *TV Century 21*
28. Brighton
29. A post-code was added
30. Jubblies

31. Vauxhall
32. The farthing
33. Billy Binns
34. The MOT test
35. Stamford Brook
36. Five pound notes
37. *The Beezer*
38. FAB
39. Chewing gum
40. Wimpy

41. 15
42. Breath tests for alcohol
43. Star ratings for petrol
44. Dennis the Menace
45. Moulton
46. Pat
47. Joe-90
48. Lion
49. Radio Luxembourg
50. Zoom

QUIZ 10

TeLevision

1. *Call My Bluff*
2. *Z Cars*
3. Dr Richard Kimble
4. *My Favourite Martian*
5. Peter Cook and Dudley Moore
6. *BBC 3*
7. The Likely Lads
8. Valerie Tatlock
9. Eamonn Andrews
10. The Cybermen

11. Oildrum Lane
12. 1968
13. *The Saint*
14. *The Virginian*
15. Millicent Martin
16. *Dixon of Dock Green*
17. *The Worker*
18. Davros
19. Stan and Hilda Ogden
20. *Rawhide*

21. William Hartnell
22. Tara King, Cathy Gale, Emma Peel
23. *Not Only – But Also*
24. Tiberius
25. *Randall and Hopkirk (Deceased)*

26. Raymond Baxter
27. Teachers
28. Wrestling
29. *Going for a Song*
30. *Gilligan's Island*

31. Her nose
32. Advertising executive
33. The Face
34. *George and the Dragon*
35. *Softly, Softly*
36. Chief Engineer Scott (Scottie)
37. *Do Not Adjust Your Set*
38. The 1966 World Cup final
39. *Crossroads*
40. Max Bygraves

41. *Please, Sir!*
42. *At Last the 1948 Show*
43. A Volvo
44. *Callan*
45. *The Telegoons*
46. Phasers
47. Napoleon Solo and Illya Kuryakin
48. West Ham
49. Jimmy Hill and Freddie Truman
50. *Miss World*

QUIZ 11

Arts and Entertainment

1. *Private Eye*
2. Allen Ginsberg
3. Ken Kesey
4. Peter Blake
5. Neil Simon
6. *Nova*
7. Rex Harrison
8. Harold Wilson and Gandhi
9. Carol Channing
10. The Establishment

11. A banana
12. Jean-Paul Sartre
13. *The Naked Ape*
14. The Booker Prize
15. Norman Mailer
16. Jack Kerouac
17. Roy Lichtenstein
18. Jacqueline Susann
19. Roald Dahl
20. Joseph Heller

21. John Fowles
22. *West Side Story*
23. *Private Eye*
24. Coventry Cathedral
25. Philip Roth
26. Roger McGough

27. *Ring of Bright Water*
28. Kurt Vonnegut Junior
29. Thor Heyerdahl
30. Joe Orton

31. Tommy Steele
32. Anthony Newley
33. *James and the Giant Peach*
34. Harper Lee
35. *Oliver!*
36. *Fiddler on the Roof*
37. Graham Greene
38. *Hair*
39. Herman Hesse

40. *One Flew Over the Cuckoo's Nest*
41. Tom Wolfe
42. *A Clockwork Orange*
43. *Naked Lunch*
44. Andy Warhol
45. David Hockney
46. *Where the Wild Things Are*

47. *Crash* (published in 1973)
48. *Pickwick*
49. Sylvia Plath
50. Ted Hughes

QUIZ 12

Sport

1. Gary Sobers
2. World Cup Willie
3. 1960 Olympics
4. Uruguay
5. Ten
6. 135,000
7. Belgian
8. Rod Laver
9. Jim Hines
10. Mary Rand

11. Sonny Liston
12. Tottenham Hotspur
13. Green Bay Packers
14. Queens Park Rangers
15. Alan Knott
16. Asia
17. Jim Clark
18. David Broome
19. Kenneth Wolstenholme
20. Barry John

21. Stirling Moss
22. Anita Lonsbrough
23. Mexico
24. The Grand National
25. Bob Beamon
26. Malcolm Nash
27. Greaves

28. Jack Charlton
29. Tommy Simpson
30. Brazil

31. Manchester City
32. Colin Cowdrey
33. Eusebio
34. Jim Clark
35. Dick Fosbury
36. Henry Cooper
37. Soviet Union and Portugal
38. Rattin
39. North Korea
40. Semi-finals

41. Gordon Banks
42. Colin Cowdrey
43. England, Scotland, Wales and Northern Ireland
44. Highbury (Arsenal)
45. Dennis Law
46. South Africa
47. Wolverhampton Wanderers (3-0)
48. Portugal, France and Argentina
49. David Hemery
50. Tottenham Hotspur

Answers

QUIZ 13

films and film stars

1. Ursula Andress
2. Elizabeth Taylor
3. *Take Me High* (made in 1973)
4. Sidney Poitier
5. Richard Burton
6. *The Odd Couple*
7. *Chitty, Chitty, Bang, Bang*
8. *Dr No*
9. *Dr Strangelove*
10. *Help!*

11. Cliff Richard and the Shadows
12. *Ben Hur*
13. Blofeld (from Bond films)
14. *Yellow Submarine*
15. *Carry On Screaming*
16. Steve McQueen
17. Tom, Dick and Harry
18. *2001: A Space Odyssey*
19. Elaine
20. *The Jungle Book*

21. *Midnight Cowboy*
22. *Dr Strangelove*
23. *Bonnie and Clyde*
24. *Goldfinger*
25. Bolivia

26. Paul Newman
27. Rooster Cogburn
28. *101 Dalmatians*
29. *Carry On Cleo*
30. *Cape Fear*

31. *The Producers*
32. *The Love Bug*
33. *It's a Mad, Mad, Mad, Mad World*
34. *Easy Rider*
35. *The Italian Job*
36. *Carry On Up the Khyber*
37. *Two Way Stretch*
38. *Planet of the Apes*
39. James Garner
40. *Mary Poppins*

41. *Sound of Music*
42. 99
43. *Breakfast at Tiffany's*
44. *A Fistful of Dollars*
45. *The Ipcress File*
46. *On Her Majesty's Secret Service*
47. *Don't Look Back*
48. *To Trap a Spy*
49. King Louie
50. *Spartacus*

QUIZ 14

Advertising and newspapers

1. Homepride
2. The *Sun*
3. Subbuteo
4. A Polar bear
5. Dulux paints
6. Smash
7. Nimble
8. Fairy Liquid
9. Bananas
10. Mouse Trap

11. Cigarettes
12. The *Sunday Mirror*
13. Fred
14. The Beatles
15. The Rolling Stones
16. Quaker Puffed Wheat
17. Colgate
18. Bournvita
19. Esso
20. Wagon Wheels

21. Milk
22. Maxwell House
23. Milk Tray
24. Fred
25. Shell

26. False
27. Birds Eye peas
28. *Thunderbirds*
29. Fry's Turkish Delight
30. Clement Freud

31. The Mini
32. The *News Chronicle*
33. Opal Fruits
34. The Wonderbra
35. Strand
36. Television sets
37. Findus
38. Sindy
39. Schweppes
40. Coca Cola

41. Carpets
42. Smarties
43. The *Daily Express*
44. Record players
45. Arthur
46. Camay
47. Brillo pads
48. *Sunday Telegraph*
49. American Express
50. Frankie Howard

QUIZ 15

TeLevision

1. *Ironside*
2. *Dad's Army*
3. Aloysius
4. *Do Not Adjust Your Set*
5. *I Dream of Jeannie*
6. Larry Hagman
7. *Lost in Space*
8. Joe-90
9. *The Prisoner*
10. Magic shows

11. *Jeux Sans Frontieres*
12. Switzerland
13. *Meet the Wife*
14. Ronnie Corbett
15. The Bonzo Dog Doo Dah Band
16. Hodges
17. *Father, Dear Father*
18. Eddie Waring
19. *Holiday 69*
20. *Doctor in the House*

21. *Monty Python's Flying Circus*
22. *On the Buses*
23. Patrick Troughton
24. Goldie Hawn
25. Hercules

26. *Sykes*
27. Oil company
28. Number 6
29. *Crossroads*
30. Tony Hancock

31. Dick Emery
32. TARDIS
33. Bill Crosby
34. Chekov
35. *The Royal Variety Performance*
36. Hawaiian Islands
37. *The Addams Family*
38. Arthur Ellis
39. Alf Garnett
40. The Dick Emery Show

41. *Steptoe and Son*
42. *The Morecombe and Wise Show*
43. *Mission Impossible*
44. Endora
45. Spike Milligan
46. Mary Whitehouse
47. *The Time Tunnel*
48. *Do Not Adjust Your Set*
49. *The Newcomers*
50. The Cooper family

QUIZ 16

Events

1. Indira Gandhi
2. Edwin 'Buzz' Aldrin
3. 1966
4. Christine Keeler
5. Mandy Rice-Davies
6. Israel
7. 1969
8. Dallas
9. Pickles
10. Ceylon (Sri Lanka)

11. Harold Wilson
12. Ian Brady
13. Czechoslovakia
14. Prince Andrew
15. Tommie Smith and John Carlos
16. 200 metres
17. London Bridge
18. Echo 1
19. D.H. Lawrence
20. Francis Chichester

21. Rudolf Nureyev
22. Malta
23. 1962
24. Trolley buses

25. Telstar
26. France
27. Sir Stanley Matthews
28. Smog
29. Charles de Gaulle
30. Britain's railways

31. Mariner 4
32. Tony Benn
33. The Kremlin
34. Harold Macmillan
35. BBC2
36. Prince Edward
37. November
38. The USSR
39. Nelson Mandela
40. Brezhnev

41. Ian Smith
42. Edward Heath
43. The moon
44. Haight-Ashbury
45. Kenya
46. Herman Titov
47. The Pope
48. Vietnam
49. High Court Judge
50. Nuclear weapons

Music

1. Tony Blackburn
2. 'Flowers in the Rain' (by the Move)
3. The Small Faces
4. Andy Warhol
5. Percy Sledge
6. Jefferson Airplane
7. Stevie Wonder
8. Dion
9. The Supremes
10. The Seekers

11. Canned Heat and King Crimson
12. Isle of Wight
13. The Band
14. Martha and the Vandellas
15. An amazing dancing bear
16. Bob Dylan
17. Dusty Springfield
18. Jagger and Richards
19. 'All You Need is Love'
20. Rod Stewart

21. Phil Spector
22. 'I'm a Believer' and 'Daydream Believer'
23. Donovan
24. Strawberry Alarm Clock
25. 'Something'
26. Pink Floyd

27. *The Velvet Underground and Nico*
28. The Archies
29. Steven Stills and Neil Young
30. *Electric Ladyland*

31. *Out of Our Heads*
32. The Temptations
33. The Spencer Davies Group, Traffic and Blind Faith
34. *From Genesis to Revelation*
35. George Harrison
36. *On Her Majesty's Secret Service*
37. Louis Armstrong
38. Billy Fury
39. 1965
40. Jefferson Airplane

41. Mary Hopkin and Badfinger
42. The Pretty Things
43. 'Dock of the Bay'
44. Bob Dylan
45. 5th Dimension
46. 'A Whiter Shade of Pale'
47. Lulu
48. Rolf Harris
49. The Kingsmen
50. The Tornados

QUIZ 18

Sport

1. Muhammad Ali
2. Jack Nicklaus
3. 1968
4. Fred Truman
5. Henry Cooper
6. Sir Alfred Ramsey
7. Alfred Di Stefano
8. Mary Rand
9. Jimmy Greaves
10. Billie Jean King

11. 100 points
12. 10,000 metres
13. Lev Yashin
14. Hampshire
15. Walter Winterbottom
16. Jim Clark
17. Ipswich Town
18. Wilma Rudolph
19. Fourth Round
20. Birmingham City

21. England 4, West Germany 2
22. 1963
23. Tottenham Hotspur
24. New Zealand (All Blacks)
25. Sonny Liston

26. 1965
27. Stanley Matthews
28. Yorkshire
29. West Ham United
30. Horse racing

31. Alan Knott
32. Wolverhampton Wanderers
33. LA Lakers
34. Celtic
35. Three times
36. West Indies
37. Jimmy Greaves
38. Australia
39. John Edrich
40. Sir Matt Busby

41. 200th time
42. 1960
43. Accrington Stanley
44. Oxford United
45. Fred Truman
46. South African
47. Gary Sobers
48. Chile
49. Jack Nicklaus
50. Neil Young

QUIZ 19

Science and Technology

1. Yuri Gagarin
2. Valium
3. John Glenn
4. Christiaan Barnard
5. Apollo 8
6. Silent Spring
7. The Forth Road Bridge
8. The Post Office Tower (GPO)
9. 1965
10. Polaroid

11. 1967
12. Michael Collins
13. Boeing 747
14. Washing machine
15. Giant Panda
16. Robots
17. Chemotherapy
18. Performed the first spacewalk
19. The computer mouse
20. Lunar Excursion Module

21. Dr Benjamin Spock
22. The felt tip pen
23. The Kiwi fruit
24. The Mig 25 jet aircraft

25. Flymo lawnmowers
26. Pulsars
27. A mobile robot
28. The Harrier
29. The Comet
30. The SR71 Blackbird

31. Pan American (Pan-Am)
32. The TSR-2
33. Fluoride
34. Japan
35. Vostok 1
36. True
37. DNA
38. Thalidomide
39. Hovercraft
40. 400

41. Cape Canaveral
42. Quartz
43. The Torrey Canyon
44. The Internet
45. Apollo 1
46. Phillips
47. South Africa
48. The M1
49. The first artificial heart transplant
50. Luna 9

QUIZ 20

Kids' Television

1. A dustbin
2. Square, round and arched
3. Deputy Dawg
4. Ermintrude
5. Green
6. *The Sooty Show*
7. Barney Rubble
8. Mr MacHenry and Mr Rusty
9. A dog
10. *The Lone Ranger*

11. Peter Purves
12. Judy
13. Jones the Steam
14. Tom
15. Primrose
16. John Noakes
17. Snagglepuss
18. *Voyage to the Bottom of the Sea*
19. *Ivanhoe*
20. Soo the Panda

21. Tom
22. *Fireball XL5*
23. Chigley
24. FAB 1
25. The Jetsons

26. Slowcoach
27. Cut-Throat Jake
28. Scott
29. Fleagle
30. Rufus Ruffcut

31. *The Arabian Knights*
32. *Crackerjack*
33. Two guide dogs for the blind
34. Double Zero
35. Red
36. An elephant
37. Officer Dibble
38. The xylophone
39. *Ivor the Engine*
40. William

41. Red
42. *Jackanory*
43. Two: Big Ted and Little Ted
44. *Vision On*
45. The Mysterons
46. *How?*
47. Skippy
48. Bunty James, Jon Miller, Fred Dineage
49. Ricky, Rebel
50. Astro

149

QUIZ 21

Music

1. Gerry and the Pacemakers
2. Paul Kantner
3. 'She's So Fine'
4. Two
5. The Supremes
6. Joni Mitchell
7. First
8. Aldous Huxley
9. *Blonde on Blonde*
10. *The White Album*

11. MC5
12. 'Lady Madonna'
13. David Jacobs
14. The Troggs
15. San Francisco
16. 'Like a Rolling Stone'
17. Love
18. Moby Grape
19. Jimi Hendrix
20. The Hollies

21. The Who
22. Desmond Dekker
23. Jane Birkin
24. Serge Gainsbourg
25. 14

26. The Rolling Stones
27. The High Numbers
28. *Magical Mystery Tour*
29. The Turtles
30. Petula Clark

31. *Let it Bleed*
32. Marty Wilde
33. Eric Burdon
34. *Mersey Beat*
35. Ian Stewart
36. 'A Whiter Shade of Pale'
37. Steve Marriot
38. Gary Puckett
39. Richmond
40. 'A Hard Rain's a Gonna Fall' and 'Masters of War'

41. MC5s
42. The Kinks
43. Jefferson Airplane
44. Helen Shapiro
45. The Shangri-Las
46. *Aftermath*
47. And the Hurricanes
48. Tony Bennett
49. Eddie Floyd
50. The McCoys

GALWAY COUNTY LIBRARIES

So You Think You Know the 70s?

Clive Gifford

So you think you know all there is to know about the seventies?

Transport yourself back to a land of macramé, mood rings and fondue sets, a land where the Raleigh Chopper and the Ford Capri were king and when you could get two fruit salad chews for a penny. Packed with questions on everything from T-Rex to tank tops, you and your friends will be able to challenge each other to remember the highs and the lows of an incredible decade.

So You Think You Know the 80s?

Clive Gifford

So you think you know all there is to know about the eighties?

Let us take you back to a time of Sinclair Spectrums, the SDP and *SuperTed*, when the pound in your pocket was made of paper and the World Wide Web was just a glint in the eye of a few visionaries. Bursting with questions on everything from Madonna to *Masters of the Universe*, rap to Roland Rat and from Delorean to *Dynasty*. Challenge your friends and test your knowledge of the yuppie-tastic 80s with this excellent new quiz book.